PSYCHODY... ...e returned on or be... CHILDREN
AND You... stamped belo...

# BASIC TEXTS IN COUNSELLING AND PSYCHOTHERAPY

Series editor: Stephen Frosh

This series introduces readers to the theory and practice of counselling and psychotherapy across a wide range of topic areas. The books appeal to anyone wishing to use counselling and psychotherapeutic skills and are particularly relevant to workers in health, education, social work and related settings. The books are unusual in being rooted in psychodynamic and systemic ideas, yet being written at an accessible, readable and introductory level. Each text offers theoretical background and guidance for practice, with creative use of clinical examples.

## Published

Jenny Altschuler
WORKING WITH CHRONIC ILLNESS

Bill Barnes, Sheila Ernst and Keith Hyde
AN INTRODUCTION TO GROUPWORK

Stephen Briggs
WORKING WITH ADOLESCENTS AND YOUNG ADULTS 2nd Edition

Alex Coren
SHORT-TERM PSYCHOTHERAPY 2nd Edition

Jim Crawley and Jan Grant
COUPLE THERAPY

Emilia Dowling and Gill Gorell Barnes
WORKING WITH CHILDREN AND PARENTS THROUGH SEPARATION AND DIVORCE

Loretta Franklin
AN INTRODUCTION TO WORKPLACE COUNSELLING

Gill Gorell Barnes
FAMILY THERAPY IN CHANGING TIMES 2nd Edition

Fran Hedges
AN INTRODUCTION TO SYSTEMATIC THERAPY WITH INDIVIDUALS

Sally Hodges
COUNSELLING ADULTS WITH LEARNING DISABILITIES

Linda Hopper
COUNSELLING AND PSYCHOTHERAPY WITH CHILDREN AND ADOLESCENTS

Sue Kegerreis
PSYCHODYNAMIC COUNSELLING WITH CHILDREN AND YOUNG PEOPLE

Ravi Rana
COUNSELLING STUDENTS

Tricia Scott
INTEGRATIVE PSYCHOTHERAPY IN HEALTHCARE

Geraldine Shipton
WORKING WITH EATING DISORDERS

Laurence Spurling
AN INTRODUCTION TO PSYCHODYNAMIC COUNSELLING 2nd Edition

Paul Terry
COUNSELLING AND PSYCHOTHERAPY WITH OLDER PEOPLE 2nd Edition

Jan Wiener and Mannie Sher
COUNSELLING AND PSYCHOTHERAPY IN PRIMARY HEALTH CARE

Shula Wilson
DISABILITY, COUNSELLING AND PSYCHOTHERAPY

Steven Walker
CULTURALLY COMPETENT THERAPY

Jessica Yakeley
WORKING WITH VIOLENCE

Invitation to authors

The Series Editor welcomes proposals for new books within the Basic Texts in Counselling and Psychotherapy series. These should be sent to Stephen Frosh at the School of Psychology, Birkbeck College, Malet Street, London, WC1E 7HX (e-mail s.frosh@bbk.ac.uk)

# PSYCHODYNAMIC COUNSELLING WITH CHILDREN AND YOUNG PEOPLE

## AN INTRODUCTION

SUE KEGERREIS

First published 2010 by
PALGRAVE MACMILLAN

Palgrave Macmillan in the UK is an imprint of Macmillan Publishers Limited, registered in England, company number 785998, of Houndmills, Basingstoke, Hampshire RG21 6XS.

Palgrave Macmillan in the US is a division of St Martin's Press LLC, 175 Fifth Avenue, New York, NY 10010.

Palgrave Macmillan is the global academic imprint of the above companies and has companies and representatives throughout the world.

Palgrave® and Macmillan® are registered trademarks in the United States, the United Kingdom, Europe and other countries

978-0-230-55196-1

This book is printed on paper suitable for recycling and made from fully managed and sustained forest sources. Logging, pulping and manufacturing processes are expected to conform to the environmental regulations of the country of origin.

A catalogue record for this book is available from the British Library.

A catalog record for this book is available from the Library of Congress.

10   9   8   7   6   5   4   3   2   1
19  18  17  16  15  14  13  12  11  10

Printed and bound in Great Britain by
CPI Antony Rowe, Chippenham and Eastbourne

*For Jacob and Sarah*

# NOTE ON CONFIDENTIALITY AND TERMINOLOGY

In this book, purely for the sake of clarity, I have written as if counsellors are female and children/clients male, unless this is clearly indicated by the material as being otherwise.

All client material included is either heavily disguised, amalgamated from more than one client or fictionalized from familiar client presentations. No client should be recognizable from any of the material described.

# CONTENTS

# ACKNOWLEDGEMENTS

I would like to thank all the students on the MSc Psychodynamic Counselling with Children and Adolescents at Birkbeck College for providing the inspiration for and some of the material in this book. In teaching them I have learned so much.

I would also like to thank my family for their patience with me during the process of writing.

# PART I

# KEY THEORIES AND TECHNIQUES

# 1

# INTRODUCTION

## The need for childhood counselling

The worrying prevalence of child and adolescent emotional difficulties is now widely recognised. The often quoted figure given by the UK Office of National Statistics 2004 is that 1 in 10 young people suffer severe mental health problems. There have also been increasing indications that disturbance is being experienced, expressed and therefore picked up by concerned adults at ever earlier stages of development. Primary school staff are receiving children aged 4 and 5 who are already significantly concerning. In January 2008, just under 150,000 children in UK primary schools were assessed as having behavioural, emotional and social difficulties – and this only covers those having Special Educational Needs status of 'school action plus' and Special Educational Needs statements. Therefore the total number of children with such difficulties is likely to be far higher (DCSF 2008). In UK national statistics and in the study by Meltzer *et al.* (2000), it has been found that 10% of boys and 5% of girls aged 5 to 10 have a mental disorder, and by the age of 11 to 16 the proportions were 13% for boys and 10% for girls.

There is much debate as to why this might be. Recent enquiries have stressed how modern society has a tendency to fail our children in providing for their emotional needs. (Children's Society 2009, Unicef 2007). Key predisposing factors identified as independently associated with increased rates of childhood mental disorders by Meltzer *et al.* (2007) ranged from 'characteristics of the child (age, sex, physical health problems, having poor scholastic achievement) to family characteristics (family structure, mother's psychological distress, poor family functioning) and household characteristics (tenure, type of accommodation and the working status of family)'. An earlier study (Meltzer *et al.* 2000) identified parental unemployment, parental psychiatric disorder, sole parenting, reconstituted

3

families, large families with more than 5 children, low income and low socio-economic status as key factors. What is clear is that families have been changing over the last few decades, which has led to an increase in instability for children through higher rates of divorce and family breakdown and changing patterns of employment. Family breakdown is a stress in itself, but in addition it is strongly associated with poverty, which UNICEF highlighted as an overriding indication of vulnerability in children (2009).

As a result of changing family structures and employment and financial pressures on family life, children are being placed in institutional care such as nurseries for longer periods and at earlier ages. Twenty-four percent of children are being brought up with a single carer, which decreases the support available to the parent and family, and this, among the other major pressures on all families to earn enough to keep going, leaves ever more children spending less time with parents. There are strong correlations between parental breakup and emotional difficulties, even if some children have the resilience to manage family breakup relatively well (Pedro-Carroll 2005). Research has shown a strong correlation between time spent by parents with their children and educational attainment (Guryan *et al.* 2008). Time spent is of course not in any simple sense a measure of relational health, but it is an indicator of the emphasis on relating in the family. Penelope Leach (2009) found that the average time spent between parent and child dropped by 40% between 1973 and 1993, although the proportion of time spent by fathers with children has increased. Parents who are physically and emotionally exhausted, busy, absent or preoccupied with coping with the practicalities of life are unable to offer children as much in both quantity and quality of interactions. There are quantitative measures of how much less verbal children are at entry into school, especially amongst the lower socio-economic groups, and while this does not itself indicate emotional problems, it is a reasonable conclusion that verbal ability has a link to the capacity to make and manage relationships and connects with how much the children have been spoken to and listened to.

Furthermore, there is solid evidence (Meltzer 2003) that there are strong continuities in the prevalence of problems. If children do not get appropriate and effective help early in life, there is a far greater likelihood that they will continue to have problems for the rest of their lives. A telling statistic is that 95% of young offenders have mental health problems (YM 2008). Eighty percent of children showing behaviour problems at 5 years of age go on to develop more serious forms of anti-social behaviour. These children need help before their problems become firmly established. As reported in *The Good Childhood Enquiry* (2009), only a quarter of children that are seriously troubled or disturbed by mental health difficulties are getting any kind of specialist help. Services offering early intervention are badly needed.

In *Every Child Matters* (DfES 2003), the importance of early intervention and support for children was stressed and agencies working with children were urged to share information and provide services to children and families. Schools are required to offer extended services in an effort to assist all children in reaching their potential. There is the potential for educational, health and social interventions to be far more integrated than before, and this gives a huge opportunity to those who want to provide counselling to troubled children. Indeed, the Institute for Public Policy Research produced a report calling for there to be a counsellor in every school (2009).

Therefore, there is not only a significant unmet need for emotional help to be given to children, but also an unprecedented opportunity for this to be delivered where the children are and at an earlier stage.

This book is intended as an introduction to the theory and practice of psychodynamic counselling with children and adolescents. It is aimed at anyone who is in a position to work therapeutically with children and adolescents – in educational settings, child and family clinics, community agencies or anywhere else where troubled young people may be reached. It is also intended to be of use to those who may not be able to offer formal counselling or other therapeutic intervention, but for whom the psychodynamic approach could prove an invaluable tool in their demanding work with emotionally damaged and difficult children or adolescents.

Working with troubled young people can be painful and difficult. They can express their difficulties in ways that test us to the limit. Whatever our role, we need to equip ourselves with enough understanding so that we can think about what the children are communicating – whether this is through their behaviour, their difficulties or their effect on us. We need to be able to understand these communications, in order to avoid getting caught in a cycle of action and reaction. We need to be able to withstand the impact on us of their emotional pain, which can otherwise cause us huge stress, leading either to a defensive retreat into 'managing cases' or becoming professionally burnt out.

The psychodynamic approach is one that can uniquely help us, not only in helping the children directly through counselling but also in providing us with a framework that can improve our perceptivity and resilience, enabling us to keep on being able to work with them, keep on understanding them, and keep on being able to offer them a receptive, thoughtful presence.

## Structure of the book – finding your way around

In Chapter 2, I will outline the key underpinning theories and concepts behind psychodynamic counselling, as it has evolved from its lineage of psychoanalysis and psychoanalytic psychotherapy. This will help the reader see how this approach helps us understand both personality and behaviour in a way that illuminates our thinking and provides tools for working with young clients. I will look at the unconscious, the inner world and containment. In relating this to the work we do, the reader is also introduced to the central ideas of transference and countertransference, as they are experienced in work with the children.

This leads on to Chapters 3 and 4, where the 'psychodynamic toolbox' is considered and described. Chapter 3 emphasizes those tools which are of use whatever the setting and whatever role we are in, while Chapter 4 concentrates on those which need to be more carefully handled, most probably in the context of the counselling room. Psychodynamic work offers a powerful set of approaches and techniques, which equip us with ways of getting more fully in touch with the children, in order thereby to help them navigate their way more successfully through whatever obstacles to development that are in their way. The psychodynamic approach also brings with it a particular view of a child's emotional development, concentrating on the processing of both the conscious and unconscious experiences at each age and stage.

In Chapter 5, I will describe a psychodynamic view of child and adolescent emotional development, with a description of the key emotional challenges of each phase. In order to understand the troubled child or adolescent in front of us, we all need a good grasp of normal child development, of the inevitable conflicts inherent in growing up, and of the ordinary difficulties, anxieties and defences arising at different ages. This will immediately help us tune in more accurately to our young client, in that we will have a greater sense of what might be at issue at this particular stage of their life. Such a dimension to our awareness is also essential so that an appropriate assessment can be made of how severe the child's difficulties may be.

Following on from this, in Chapter 6 there is a deeper look at the challenges of learning. This is central to the task of growing up, and is the arena in which so many children and adolescents experience frustration and failure. As many counsellors work in schools and universities, it is likely to be a key feature in those referred for help, even if the underlying emotional dynamics are manifesting themselves in many other areas of the young person's life. A detailed understanding of how difficult and complex learning can be is crucial for anyone working with children or adolescents. There is, in addition, a direct connection between what makes learning difficult and what might get between the child and the potential benefits of counselling. As a result, this section also has a bearing on some of the dynamics around getting help that are likely to be aroused in the counselling itself.

Then we move on in Chapter 7 to a more detailed look at the tools of the trade, that is the use of play and art materials in work with children and adolescents. This is one area where the work can differ fundamentally from similar work with older age groups. Anyone working with younger children (although adolescents can also often make good use of art materials) needs to be able to understand play as communication and to interpret what is being expressed symbolically through art. We not only need to be able to pick up on what is being expressed in these ways, but also to be able to know what to do with this in the counselling room. We need to know how to play with the child in a way that is facilitating and helpful, which requires the capacity to have one foot in the game and one outside it, to be able to think and comment but also to take part.

Working with children has many differences from working with adults, and one key difference is in the area of difficult behaviour. Children's problems will often not be something that they can describe and talk about, nor even something that they are able to play or draw about. They can only be acted out and dramatized through behaviour. In Chapter 8, I describe some of the challenges children can present in the work, and ways of thinking about responses. While adults can become violent, storm out, or otherwise break the boundaries of what is usually a talking encounter, children will much more frequently present challenging or disturbing behaviour that has to be managed by the counsellor. A psychodynamic counsellor has to find a way to respond that is constructive rather than punitive, thoughtful rather than retaliatory. Sometimes this will be through insightful interpretation, which will help the child stop the behaviour as he will feel understood, but for others this will be through appropriate limit-setting. Psychodynamic work is to do with understanding the meaning behind behaviour of whatever sort, and if difficult behaviour is managed well, then not only is the setting preserved, but the child is given a direct example of being contained, both in thought and action, without that meaning being denied.

Whenever we work with children and adolescents we are always highly conscious of the family behind them. Our understanding of the child and their relationship with us will be informed by a growing grasp of the family dynamics that have underpinned the child's emotional development. The family is also the child's first 'group' and many of their ways of coping with – or failing to cope with – group life will have their roots in their family experiences. Children are in groups for much of their lives, and some have serious difficulties in group settings while being able to cope better in one-to-one encounters. Both for this reason, and because working therapeutically with groups can be beneficial for so many children, Chapter 9 looks at psychodynamic group work and group dynamics.

One of the other major differences between working with children and adolescents as opposed to adults is around issues of consent. Children and adolescents are most often sent to counselling by someone else, and it is often far from clear who the actual client is. The counsellor is not in simple dyad with the young person, but is more often in a complex constellation with either school or family or both. This requires professionalism and skill in the counsellor, and Chapter 10 explores some of the complexities around consent and contract in this work. It also considers some of the skills needed to engage the child or adolescents themselves so that, whoever the referrer, the young person becomes an active client on their own behalf.

Another area that can raise difficulties about being able to give and receive help is around the differences between counsellor and client. It is a truism in work with children that there is always going to be one difference – age – which sets up its own dynamic. However, there are also often going to be differences in ethnicity, gender, class, physical and mental ability, and life chances. With older children and adolescents, differences in terms of sexual orientation may also need to be carefully considered. Chapter 11 looks at the psychodynamic view of these issues and gives some idea of how to take up such issues productively in the work. We need to be aware of who we are in the children's eyes, even before the actual therapeutic relationship has a chance to develop, if we are to under-stand and be able to work with the relationship in the room. We need to know how these both real and perceived differences between the child and others are making an impact in his life, and to have some understanding of the way in which they shape the child's experience of his world. We also need to be alert to our own difficulties in the area of difference, and to be aware of how much work we might need to do within ourselves to remain fully available to the client.

Most counsellors working with children and adolescents are going to be working in organizational settings. If we are to be effec-tive, we will need to understand the institutional framework within which we are practising and also that within which the children are living and experiencing their difficulties. We need to appreciate the way in which they and we are fitting in with or being acted upon by dynamics that are much larger than the individual. Otherwise we can be prone to misunderstand the pressures on them or interpret as purely personal issues that are part of the whole institution's way of functioning. Each setting will provide its own context to the work that will have a powerful effect on both the counsellor and the child's experience of the work.

In Chapters 12 and 13, I provide an outline of the particular issues, opportunities and constraints offered in some typical settings. This will also highlight some differences between coun-selling and psychotherapy, as the context in which the work is offered has a crucial impact on the style of work that will be appro-priate. The setting will always raise issues around relationships with other staff, confidentiality, the sharing of the counsellor with other clients, the attitude of the institution towards the counselling, and of the place of counselling in the client's mind. All these need to be understood and to be central in our thinking if we are to manage ourselves and the work professionally and make the most of the opportunities to help these particular children in this particular setting.

Thus far nothing explicit has been mentioned about the amount of time a child or adolescent may be in counselling. One of the differences often identified between counselling and psychotherapy is that the latter is usually longer-term. Open-ended or fairly long-term counselling is offered in many settings, but in some agencies and some circumstances it is required or recommended that the child or adolescent be offered short-term or time-limited coun-selling. In Chapter 14, I consider psychodynamic ideas useful in regard to such work. Issues around time are always strongly present in work with young people, as their own developmental and educational imperatives impinge on them and on the counselling. In schools the structure of the school year is always imposing its own rhythm, and the external pressures of exams and transitions from primary to secondary school, or from school to college, are always integral to the work. Furthermore, there is much to be gained from developing a skill in psychodynamic therapeutic interventions that can be short, as there are often times when a brief, focused piece of understanding can free up a young person who has become blocked by some developmental or emotional obstacle, enabling them to move on after limited intervention. Especially in adolescence, this can be a way for them to make use of help without becoming attached in an intimate relationship just as they are moving away from such dependence in their outside lives.

One of the crucial but sometimes neglected tasks for any counsellor meeting a new child or adolescent is to conduct a careful assessment, whether or not an explicit session or number of sessions is labelled as such. This is both to assess the suitability of the case for counselling input, including a risk assessment, and also to inform the style and direction of the work, if undertaken. Chapter 15 outlines central questions that need to be asked in the assessment phase, so that both counsellor and client can be sure that the work offered is appropriate and the beginnings of an understanding can be established. A good assessment can lay the foundations for focused and sensitive work, enhance engagement and ensure that the counsellor is making an informed choice about what is being offered, why and how it is going to be most effective.

In the final chapter, I will look at dynamics around ending a counselling relationship, both for the child but also for the family and referrers. For all children, but especially for those who have experienced powerful losses and separations in their lives, ending a relationship well can be of immense importance. Counselling gives a unique opportunity to work on what separation can mean and help children with their feelings of loss. However, endings cannot always be managed smoothly because children might leave abruptly for new schools, or other factors extraneous to the counselling might interfere with crucial final sessions. This chapter looks at some of the emotional dynamics around endings, managing expectations, formally gathering feedback and building a much-needed evidence base for the work. Consideration is given to both formal and informal feedback channels, which can be used to evaluate the counselling process. Feedback can be carefully and sensitively built into the ending process so as to bring a review element into the work, both in the interests of a good ending and in the interests of providing support for this approach.

There is a great need at a national level to address the wider underlying causes of the rising levels of distress in children and adolescents (*Good Childhood Enquiry* 2009). There are major societal and political issues that have a bearing on childhood emotional well-being. However, while we may campaign to have these addressed in the longer term, we can offer some immediate help with their difficulties through the provision of sensitive and skilled practitioners. We need to go out to where the children are to provide this service, offering them help at an early stage, before the problems become woven into their personalities for the rest of their lives.

# 2

# KEY THEORETICAL IDEAS IN PSYCHODYNAMIC THINKING

Psychodynamic thinking has its origins in psychoanalysis. Freud's original formulation of psychoanalysis, both as a way of understanding human development and its vicissitudes, and as a method of treatment for psychological difficulties, has been refined, elaborated and extended by different writers and practitioners who have applied his models and systems in ever richer ways. In this chapter, some of the key ideas underpinning the psychodynamic approach are outlined, to clarify its main features and in so doing briefly indicate how it differs from other possible orientations.

The central concepts that have been chosen are the unconscious, the inner world and containment. These to me are the ones that most help us delineate what is particular about the psychodynamic approach, in terms of understanding both how people work and what can be therapeutic when we try to help them. In describing these ideas I will also be bringing in the terms transference and countertransference. These are usually put forward as key concepts in themselves, and indeed they are without doubt essential components of the psychodynamic approach, but they make more sense in the context of the others than if put forward on their own.

## The unconscious

Central to the psychodynamic way of thinking is the notion that we are guided in our actions, feelings, choices and ways of relating to others by factors of which we are not consciously aware. Our rational, conscious selves can only do so much to be in control of what we do and even of how we perceive things. It is a near universal experience for people to promise themselves not to repeat a pattern of damaging behaviour, whether it is something big, like falling in love with the 'wrong' kind of partner or something more mundane like raiding the fridge one more time or having that one drink too many. We are all propelled to do things we know are unhelpful to us, to repeat patterns that have already been seen not to work well before, despite the best intentions of our conscious selves. We all know that there are many conflicts within us that mean that different parts of ourselves take control at different times. In the case of the over-eating example, it may be that both parts are in one sense conscious – that is that 'we don't think we should' but 'we want to' and we are aware of both, so this does not seem like an issue about the unconscious at all. However, as well as there being the accessible difficulties over self-control, the underlying motivation that sabotages our efforts to stay slim and healthy may be deeply unconscious (Bruch 1974; Orbach, 1978) and/or the anxieties that we are perhaps keeping at bay by over-eating are unconscious. In the deeper cases of the choice of partner, we tend not to realize that we are in a repetitive pattern until much later in the process, when the unconscious dynamics of love and desire have overpowered not only our actions but our perceptions (Scharff 1982; Ruszcinsky 1993).

The psychodynamic way of understanding this is to emphasize that from very early in our lives we are deeply influenced by what happens to us and by the emotional atmosphere around us. Long before we can think in words or remember in our thoughts, we are being formed by our physical and emotional experiences. Patterns and emotional repertoires are being laid down right from the beginning, as what will be our selves is shaped and forged by the unique emotional world that surrounds us. We learn who we are through our intimate experiences with others, and we learn about how to be with others through those earliest relationships.

Most of these processes and their outcomes are unconscious. We do not have to think about our infant experiences or remember them in thought to be deeply influenced by them. As little babies, as elucidated and emphasized in the work of Melanie Klein (1959), we are helpless and exposed to great anxieties and terrors, and we have to cope with being dependent on someone else for everything we need. However well our parents do what they can to help us through this amazingly intense time (to offer a 'facilitating environment' – Winnicott 1963), we will all have had to defend ourselves against some of the terrors, and will all have devised ways of dealing with how difficult it is to be dependent on someone else for our emotional and physical well-being. For the luckiest amongst us, our parents will have offered us something sufficiently consistent, loving and enriching to leave us still able to be open, honest, emotionally available and ready for learning, life and experience. However, for each and every one of us, that will have been jeopardized to a greater or lesser extent by our need to defend ourselves against a range of difficult experiences, and at times overwhelming anxieties.

Those who have been faced with hostile, majorly conflicted or inconsistent parenting, who have, for whatever reason, been exposed to more anxiety than could be managed, and whose distress was perhaps not picked up or could not be attended to adequately, will have built up a range of unconscious defences that at the time helped them cope, but later in life make it difficult to use their minds, to make the most of themselves and to make good, satisfying relationships. These defences are not conscious, or chosen. The child who becomes unmanageably hostile whenever faced with something he does not already know, or the adolescent who is compelled to cut herself rather than feel her rage and helplessness, are not acting from free rational choice. They are being propelled by unconscious forces and old defences built up long ago to help protect against early difficulties. It is this layer of our minds, buried in the unconscious, which is the focus of psychodynamic work.

## The inner world

The second concept that has been chosen as central to psychodynamic thinking is 'the inner world'. In a way this has already been alluded to, because the inner world is all in the unconscious realm. But using this concept extends the thinking about the unconscious in an important way. By the 'inner world' is meant the array of experiences, ways or 'schemas of being with others' (Stern 1995b) and 'ways of experiencing others' that has been laid down inside us as we grew up.

This inner world is not just a carbon copy of what actually happened to us, as we are not just passive recipients of experience, even when we first set out in life. Our parents are not just printing themselves on the blank sheet of us in our babyhood. We as babies, later as children and adolescents and into adulthood, shape our own experiences. Each baby is born different, with differing capacities for managing frustration, different levels of alertness with which to engage with the outside world, different abilities to manage internal and external sensations. These will deeply affect how we experience the efforts our parents make to provide for our needs, and their failures in doing so. Our state of mind and state of development will have a vital role in how we experience things. We build up our inner worlds, not just out of what happens, but out of what we make of what happens. What for one hungry baby might be felt to be a manageable wait for a feed may be for another experienced as catastrophic abandonment and attack from within. It is not just the events, but the meanings of the events that have an effect on us. This is also cumulative, in that we experience new events through the emotional lenses already established for us, and so we can misperceive and misinterpret, as well as perceive and interpret what is happening.

This highlights another crucial aspect of this concept of the inner world, in that we carry it around with us and impose it on the world we find ourselves in. This can be illustrated by the way that for many of us there is a particular character or relationship that keeps turning up in our world, no matter where we go. As an example of this, Helen has an 'older sister' character whom she is continually finding. To Helen – as this is what she made of having an older sister in her particular family dynamic – she appears to be someone who 'got there' earlier, has everything worked out already, and has used up all the emotional energy before Helen arrives. Moreover, if Helen tries to work alongside her, she is bound to be caught up in a rivalrous conflict which Helen will lose. After considerable time in counselling Helen can now deal with this character a lot better than she used to; she is no longer crowded out by her or as driven into unhelpful competitiveness or despairing defeatism as easily as before. She can recognize what she is doing when she finds herself in a familiar emotional place and can stop herself from falling into familiar traps. However, the fact remains that this sister character still might re-emerge at any moment.

Someone might say that the reappearance of this figure in Helen's life is just bad luck. Others who understand that this scenario has unconscious roots might suggest that her early take on her experience leads her to misperceive people in this way and that the next new candidate for this 'sister' figure is not really like that – all Helen needs to do is realize that she is shaped by Helen's imagination and being seen wrongly by her. This latter is indeed an important part of what the psychodynamic approach would suggest. The vital extra ingredient that takes this further is the idea that, if Helen does not happen to find someone much like this sister immediately available, she will 'create' someone. She will unconsciously place someone in that role, and put out lots of unconscious messages that will subtly push this chosen person into playing that role in her life. This person would of course have to be emotionally available for this, and we choose carefully those we elect into these positions and select only those likely to play their part.

We all have our cast of characters in our inner worlds, and we not only tend to react to people as if they conform to one of them, but we also put a lot of unconscious effort into pushing people into these roles. It is for this reason that our relationships so often end up following familiar patterns, even when we have sworn to ourselves that this time it will be different. It is not just that we repeatedly choose the same sort of people to be our 'partners in psychodynamic crime', but also we unconsciously give them the script we need them to follow. We are compelled to repeat (Freud 1920), unless we can find a way of uncovering the unconscious patterns.

This can be further illustrated by some examples. Carol, 13, came to see the school counsellor because she was getting into increasingly violent rows with her classmates. She was seen as a bully. When Carol met the counsellor she explained how she felt picked on, laughed at and ostracized by the other girls, who teased her and made remarks about her mother, who died several years ago. There are many ways one could approach this situation. One could try to help her learn anger control techniques, or teach her how to avoid provocative situations. One could help her look at her faulty thinking, in which she clearly experienced a much closer link than was there between their taunts and her actual home situation of which her tormentors knew little. But for a psychodynamic counsellor what would be a more useful strategy would be to explore with Carol her feelings around her mother's death, her anger and resentment at her peers who have living mothers, and her fury at the deprivation both emotional and material (father did not work and relied on income support). Some of this was openly available to conscious thought, of course, but it was not consciously at work in her mind when she got into fights, which to her were always justified by the immediate situation.

However, there was more uncovered, as the work went deeper. It was discovered that Carol was not only angry with her mother for dying and leaving her, but also felt worthless and bad, as if deep down she felt that her mother died because she was not good enough to stay alive for. Every time her peers taunted her it tapped into an unconscious fear and deep hurt that she was indeed rubbish. This robbed her of any ordinary robustness that could cope with teasing. It was discovered that her mother drank heavily and was erratic, sometimes loving but often neglectful and angry. This helped towards the understanding that Carol's paranoid vigilance, accompanied by the constant fear that her friends were always on the point of turning into enemies, was a reliving of some very early experiences.

As this process of understanding progressed, Carol began to see how much she contributed to the difficulty in her relationships, and began to discriminate much better how people were responding to her, and to be able to walk away from provocation. She began to realize how she unconsciously provoked others into being persecutory and how much she was using them to fight old battles. She managed more often to stop herself becoming provocative, and stopped herself also getting into rows on behalf of other children she thought were being badly treated and therefore identified with. As she became less often on hyper-red alert, her friendships became less fraught and her periods of calm become longer. The battles she had been fighting were ones rooted in early experiences, and were being inflamed by unconscious connections that ensured that the pattern had to continue. By uncovering these elements she regained control over herself and began to address the self-destructiveness that had been threatening her whole future.

Another example is Akeem, 15, who was referred for counselling because he was constantly getting into trouble with teachers whom he saw as picking on him. He was full of the unfairness of why he was identified and punished when he 'isn't doing anything the others haven't done'. When he finally drove a teacher to eject him he felt a mixture of triumph at having really got to her and a fury at her unjustness. What emerged in the counselling is that his father left the family long ago and his mother was barely coping. He had a difficult combination of contempt for his mother and a worried fear over how vulnerable she was and how damaged she seemed. In the counselling it became clear that underneath the conscious feeling of how much he despised the teachers, he was at the same time longing for them to be able to manage him without recourse to panic and tears. Akeem maybe did not do much that the 'others haven't done' in some practical ways, but he was posing a challenge to the teachers that got to them in a way that the others did not. There was more at stake. Would it be Akeem or they who felt humiliated, worthless and needy? He both wanted them to be able to stand up to him and also to bear all the horrible feelings of being no good and unworthy. So he felt compelled to provoke them, as indeed he did his mother. Buried far down was a small boy who needed his mother to be stronger than she was, to reassure him that he was not too much for her, that his father had not left because he was too much for him. Akeem's hatred of neediness and his longing for a strong adult was manifested in difficult behaviour in class. He was effectively recruiting his teachers to become his father who rejected him, and to become his mother who could not cope with him.

## Containment

The third concept that I have chosen to typify the psychodynamic approach is containment. So far I have written of psychodynamic ways of understanding the individual and the way their inner worlds become so powerful in affecting their relationships, rather than psychodynamic ways of helping when things have already gone wrong. Discussion of containment takes us into this latter territory.

Containment as a word has different meanings, and can be used just to mean limit-setting or constraint (see Miller-Pietroni 1999 for a consideration of the range of uses). We can be said to contain diffi-cult behaviour when we make rules and impose sanctions. We can be said to contain someone if we hold them so they cannot hit us. In the psychodynamic world it means something else. It is a word applied to what a good mother does when she feels her baby's distress and anxiety, his or her fear that s/he is about to fall apart or be overwhelmed (Bion 1962a). If the mother herself is psychically strong, she will take the baby's feeling on board, sort it out inside herself and transform it into something that helps her understand and take appropriate action to ease the baby's panic. However, if she is herself feeling overwhelmed, she might feel totally panicked herself, or might retaliate with anger, or she might just switch off and refuse even to take in how her baby is feeling.

As we work as a psychodynamic counsellor with a client, some-thing similar to this maternal function is called for. We have to keep thinking and trying to understand whatever is going on, even if the feelings aroused are strong and difficult. We have to try to under-stand what the client is communicating, whether in words, actions, way of relating or the way they are making us feel. All these elements need to be processed and taken fully on board, even when that includes their experience of us as unhelpful or hostile. How they experience and deal with us needs itself to be seen as a communication of their inner world. We need to look at ourselves all the time to see how the client might be recruiting us into their cast of characters to play a part in their private drama.

For example, the counsellor with Akeem described above had to experience and feel belittled by his scorn for her before she could fully understand what was going on between him and the adults around him. She had to manage her own feeling that she was useless and, indeed, her own wish to be relieved of having to deal with him, before the strength of his inner conviction that he was worthless and more than could be coped with could come through clearly for understanding. The scenario he was carrying around inside him was repeated in the counselling room, and could then be worked with because she could think about it rather than simply act the part given to her. As Ann Alvarez (1992, p. 4) writes, '... brave, receptive listening, and a firm and not too masochistic attitude to the child's possible quite horrible projections – that is, to the child's desperate need to do to us what he feels was done to him – do seem to help.'

## Transference

Although transference and countertransference have not yet been explicitly focused on, they are central to what has already been said above. Psychodynamic counsellors will always be trying to attend to and understand the particular flavour of and developments in the relationship between them and their clients, as a key way of seeing the client's inner world in action. The transference is a term used for the way our clients see us and react to us, as if we are the figures they have in their inner world. We need always to be trying to process how we are being perceived by the client and who we are for them; this can then be used as a way of understanding how the client's inner world is influencing his relationships both within the room and outside. It is a direct route into understanding the way in which the people around him become recruited into his inner drama again and again. Our task is to notice this in action and transform it into something that informs us whether and how to intervene. This could lead to something being said, something being done or just in thoughtful silence. We can sometimes see quite easily the nature of the transference, in a way that stays quite clear of our own sensations – for example, when a child is fearful that we are going to disapprove of messiness when this is simply not the case. However, there are other times when the route to understand what is going on in the transference is only through how the client makes us feel, and how we find ourselves driven to respond and behave.

## Countertransference

This brings us to the final key concept that I want to introduce – the countertransference. During the work with a difficult or troubled child we might feel an urge to retaliate, or to be pushed into inappropriate actions, such as rushing to the rescue, meaningless reassurance or forceful advice. We might feel hopeless, angry, confused or bored. It is vital to monitor how we ourselves are feeling, as a way of working out more clearly what the transference is – what kind of relationship is being made and enacted between us and the client.

This is where containment truly comes in, as we have to manage our anxiety, our anger, our confusion, and do something like what a mother does, by trying to bear the feelings, and hopefully process them and understand. By working on and using the countertransference we are doing something powerful. Firstly, we are managing to stay thoughtful rather than unthinkingly taking up the position dictated by the child's inner world, and therefore we are offering the child someone who will not play the part given to them, perhaps for the first time. Secondly, we are endeavouring to process the feelings and the emotional currents that are too much for the child to manage. If we can work this through, we may be able to hand it back to the child as a piece of understanding that can be consciously wrestled with, rather than a pattern that will unconsciously repeat itself over and over again.

Containment means being aware of and managing our own feelings, noticing and absorbing the anxieties and difficulties of the child, and processing the transference and the countertransference. It means the working out and working through of the child's inner world as it gets enacted in the room and in the relationship. As a psychodynamic counsellor, more than anything else we offer our understanding of our clients' inner worlds, hard won through direct experience and observation of the way the relationship works in the counselling. This enables the clients gradually to allow changes into their inner worlds as different experiences filter through their defences and establish new possibilities. They become more conscious of what is underlying their perceptions, behaviour and choices, and thereby gain more control over what they are doing and greater emotional availability and stability.

This places us as counsellors in an extremely central position in the work, and requires deep self-knowledge. It is difficult and demanding, because we are not there to give the clients a prescription of how to behave, or trying straightforwardly to teach them how to manage better. The main tool is our selves, and the main arena for the work is in the here and now, in what happens between us and the client. We have to be extremely self-aware in order to become more sure how much is our own and how much the client's. We have to be open to difficult and painful feelings, and use them in the service of understanding the client better. We have to have done the necessary work on our own unconscious in personal therapy if we are to have the capacity to bear what is given to us to bear, and to be able to perceive clearly what we need to perceive.

We also all need skilled supervision in order to help us process the experience of being with the children. The ability to recognize, understand and make use of transference and countertransference in our encounters with clients grows slowly, and we need someone outside ourselves to help us become more adept. Supervisors help us understand the children better through their greater experience of children's difficulties and communications, but in psychodynamic work they crucially also help us to step back and reflect sufficiently to see how we ourselves are being acted on by the children's inner worlds.

Armed with these theoretical tools – an understanding of the unconscious and the inner world – the psychodynamic counsellor can offer the child containment. We can use our ongoing perceptions of the transference and countertransference to gain insight into what is driving the child into unhelpful emotional and relational constellations and to offer them a route away from constant repetition of old patterns. The ways in which we can translate these crucial elements of understanding into helpful techniques are the subject of the next chapter.

# 3
# KEY ELEMENTS OF
# PSYCHODYNAMIC TECHNIQUE 1

## Introduction

One of the beauties of psychodynamic understanding is that it can be used to underpin the employment of a wide variety of techniques. Psychodynamic counselling itself uses techniques that have their roots in psychotherapy and psychoanalysis, and these will be described below, but a psychodynamically informed practitioner can also harness his or her understanding to the effective employment of many other kinds of intervention. The psychodynamic theoretical framework provides a way of perceiving the deeper levels of what is going on within and between people, and of how someone is experiencing themselves in relation to others. It can then guide us in our choices, even if we are not in a setting where psychodynamic counselling itself would be appropriate (Clare Winnicott 1955; Dyke 1984). For example, a teacher or social worker has a different role from that of a counsellor, but she can still use her psychodynamic understanding to help her respond to what is really going in the child, rather than react to the surface manifestations. A practitioner who is using cognitive behavioural techniques or offering problem-solving strategies is going to be much better equipped to devise useful interventions if they are in touch with the underlying communications in children's behaviour or ways of relating. This chapter and the next will look at a range of techniques concentrating on those that are most basic – and therefore the most flexible and available to be used in a range of settings – through to those which find their place in formal counselling.

# Techniques used in the psychodynamic approach

There are two guiding principles behind psychodynamic psychotherapy and psychoanalysis: firstly, that improvements in a client's life follow changes in the client's inner world, and secondly, that improvements will imply a more open interplay between inner and external worlds. Regarding the former, the client is enabled to make progress through shifts in the nature of the characters that inhabit their inner world and the quality of relationships between them. Changes in behaviour and improved functioning in the outside world are brought about by inner changes that enable the client to have kindlier and more helpful internal resources to call on with less likelihood of inner destructiveness and persecution. In relation to the latter, there also needs to be a richer and more flexible 'conversation' between the inner world and the external world, so that the individual's perceptions of others are more genuinely attuned to how these others really are, rather than being too readily assumed to fit one of the internal templates that have in the past been so powerful in engendering distortions. In Chapter 2, I described the way in which perceptions and relationships are influenced by the way in which the inner world is imposed on and gets between us and the external world.

The psychoanalytic terms for the mechanisms involved in these distortions are projection and projective identification. The first refers to when we attribute to others feelings that are in fact our own, without this necessarily having any effect on them. Thus I might perceive someone as hostile when in fact I am feeling hostility that I don't want to acknowledge, but the recipient of the projection need not be influenced at all by my projection. The second is the way in which we exert effective pressure on others to carry elements of our inner world and induce them to play parts in our inner drama, as described in Chapter 2. In counselling we seek to diminish the extent to which these mechanisms dominate the client's relationships. In ordinary language this will mean that the individual is able to relate to others more as they are, rather than either experiencing them in a distorted way or coercing them into behaving like their inner cast of characters.

This kind of change can happen in ordinary life through helpful relationships with others that enable us to experience the world with greater freedom and richness. However, by definition, many of the children and adolescents that come for counselling have impoverished or damaged inner worlds. This makes it difficult for them to recognize or make good use of the potentially nurturing relationships around them. Furthermore, as indicated in the previous chapter, the unconscious compulsion to recreate their inner drama steers them into relationships that exacerbate the damage.

In psychodynamic counselling the changes in the inner world and the relationship between inner and outer realities are brought about through the client's lived experience of the relationship with the counsellor. The driving force for change is grounded in the development of insight – first perhaps the counsellor's but essentially in the later stages the client's – into the unconscious forces at work. With smaller children and in some contexts the insight may never be explicitly articulated, but the quality of the relationship will be mediated by the counsellor's capacity to understand and respond to the unconscious roots of the client's difficulties and to process the experience of being with the client through these difficulties. The lived experience of being with someone who is in tune with the child's emotional reality and available for the reworking of relationships that have gone wrong in the past enables the child to readdress old conflicts and dismantle old defences. They can thereby install different inner objects in their internal worlds and discover the capacity for different kinds of connections between them and others and change their relationship with themselves.

These ways of working therefore do not involve the giving of advice, reassuring the client or directly working to boost their self-esteem. The psychodynamic work is primarily done through the client's free associations – i.e. the thoughts, fantasies and feelings that are spontaneously generated in the client's mind – as it is through them that the unconscious can be revealed and the relationship allowed to take its distinctive shape – one which will be unique to each therapeutic pair. In children these free associations will only rarely be verbal, and they will more usually take the form of play, use of art materials and behaviour, all of which articulate the conscious and unconscious links and connections the child is making.

Using this approach, the psychodynamic counsellor will normally let the child or adolescent 'lead' the sessions. Within established safe boundaries (see Chapter 8 for consideration of behaviour and limit-setting) they will follow the child in whatever he does, commenting where helpful. They will not usually impose a framework or an agenda, but will let the client talk or play or use art materials as they choose. This enables them to find out what is really going on in the child's mind, rather than steer the work to where the counsellor's own thoughts and preoccupations might be heading.

There are two different types of tools that psychodynamic coun-sellors have at their disposal, the practical and the technical. The practical tools comprise the equipment needed to provide a coun-selling experience for the child. I will start with this, as it provides the backdrop for the work but, as will be made clear, the materials we provide are far less important than the techniques by which we make explicit to the child our mental space and emotional availability.

## Practical equipment

Younger children receiving psychodynamic counselling need to be provided with materials that enable them to express their emotional reality. Toys, such as animal families, a dolls' house, dolls large and small, fences, cars, and so on will enable relationship play to develop. Modelling material, drawing and/or painting equipment, scissors, string and tape are extremely useful. In many traditions, a therapist would provide the child with a box of toys that is theirs alone, not shared with any other child. This is helpful, as the child can build up a totally personal world in their box. But for many of us this is not practicable and materials will have to be shared. However, even if most of the equipment is shared it is helpful if each child can have a box in which to keep things they have made or pictures they have drawn. There are undoubtedly disadvantages to having to share equipment, as other children can use, lose or spoil what your client wants (and he will have the power to do the same). As a result, physical continuity between sessions is much harder to maintain. However, sharing equipment can correspondingly bring rapidly to the surface issues important in sibling and school rela-tionships, such as jealousy, envy and competition. Other children are more 'present' as part of the relationship between child and counsellor, which can provide useful opportunities to consider the difficulties that arise in relation to these others, both in reality and fantasy.

It is not helpful to provide too much in the room. Deprived chil-dren, walking into a lavishly equipped room replete with every toy or game they can imagine can find it provocative and seductive. It may then be harder for the child to use the materials to express what is in their mind, and will make it more difficult for the inner sense of deprivation to surface in the room. Excitement, envy and resentment may be aroused, as the room becomes then a represen-tative of all they do not normally have.

What matters in choosing equipment is whether it is likely to enhance or inhibit emotional expression, and whether it is flexible rather than in some way dictating how it will be used. Most board games for example can easily be used defensively and as a barrier rather than an aid to communication. Some counsellors find it helpful to have books in the room that explore emotional themes and others have puppets with a range of characters and expressions, through which the children can enact scenarios that they could not otherwise put into words. It is helpful to have soft as well as hard toys, and some homely and potentially comforting touches such as blankets and cushions.

Adolescents may well be put off if they enter a counselling room filled with younger children's equipment, as they are often hyper-alert to any sign that they are not being treated as having left child-hood behind. Paper and pencils/pens and a few other props such as scissors and tape can be usefully left within reach. However, it is often helpful to have a few 'younger' pieces of equipment (such as plasticine or a sand-tray) in the farther reaches of the room so that the adolescent can use them if they wish, as once they have relaxed somewhat and have begun to be more in touch with their younger selves, there are some who relish the opportunity to use them.

The toys and other equipment need careful thought, but they are the props rather than the true tools of the work. These are of a different nature, as it is through the counsellor's thinking and ways of managing the relationship that the real work is done.

## The psychodynamic toolbox

The psychodynamic tools the counsellor has at his or her disposal are relatively few, but they are very powerful.

## *Observation*

The first tool that will always be to hand is observation. All psycho-dynamic practitioners have had, as part of their training, the oppor-tunity to develop the capacity for psychodynamic observation. The ideal is to have honed this skill through infant observation (Miller *et al.* 1989, Reid 1997; Sternberg 2005) where a baby and their carer are observed for an hour weekly from birth onwards for at least a year, and an account of the observation is discussed in seminars. The role of observer is one in which one simply takes in what is going on, without helping, intervening or playing any other active part in the scenario. This gives the student a chance to observe first-hand the primitive layers of early emotional life which underpin so much of our functioning, particularly our difficulties, and to witness the emotionally intense and subtle interactions that form the bedrock of our relatedness from birth. However, even more importantly perhaps, it teaches the counsellor-to-be how to see and perceive emotional interactions more clearly and be alert to their own emotional responses. It helps to develop their ability to observe, truly to notice and take in what is going on in the infant/carer dyad, and from there to be far more alert to what is going on in the client. It serves to develop the 'capacity to tolerate anxiety, uncertainty and a sense of bombardment' (Sternberg 2005), which enables the counsellor to continue to be perceptive even if in the presence of intense emotional events. It enables the counsellor to develop their ability to identify imaginatively with the emotional reality of both carer and baby, which helps equip them with the capacity to empathize with and appreciate the unique emotional forces at work for each individual. Hinshelwood and Skogstad (2000, p. 18) describes the function of observation as being 'to hone their intuitive sensitivity to human experiences and situations and to begin to develop a psychoanalytic attitude in which one retains, feels and thinks about the experience of the other, the observed, without an immediate recourse to acting on the internal and external pressures.'

If infant observation is out of reach of the student, then similar capacities can still be effectively developed by pursuing other kinds of observation, in nurseries or playgroups, in the school playground or in ordinary everyday settings. It is also best pursued in the context of a seminar where the rest of the group can offer containment to the observer, notice elements, particularly unconscious dimensions, of the observation that the observer has not been able to register and help the observer with the difficulties of their role. The same requirements pertain, though; one needs simply to observe, not to be actively engaged. It is easy to underestimate how much practice and hard work it takes to become an effective psychodynamic observer, as observing sounds like a passive exercise, but in fact it is a skill in itself, which needs to be worked on and honed and never taken for granted.

In psychodynamic work, using the ability to observe in this emotionally open way and to 'think under fire' (Bion 1982), we can watch to see what the child client does, how he does it, what feelings he conveys and what feelings he evokes. We will try to take in all the little details of how he plays, how he holds himself, how he looks at or doesn't look at us, how he uses the room and the equipment. Even if nothing is said, we will, simply by looking carefully, convey a particular kind of interest in the child that may be therapeutic in itself. Playing in the presence of this kind of observing other is a very different experience from playing on one's own or with someone who is more interested in their own agenda.

For example, Paulie, aged 6, came into the counselling room without looking at the counsellor. He dashed over to the dolls' house and grabbed all the contents with both hands, flinging them onto the table. He pulled all the soft toys off the shelf and left them in a heap. Meanwhile the counsellor sat and watched, wondering why he was in such a state. She paid careful attention to his body language, as he threw his arms around and yet seemed floppy and uncoordinated. She noticed that even though he seemed quite wild, out of the corner of his eye he was himself noticing her watching, so she stayed calm and waited to see what happened next. She thought about the fact that he had missed the last session, having gone away for the weekend to see his father whom he rarely visited, and that he had not returned in time to come back to school on Monday, although no-one knew why. She began to think about how much of a mess he might be feeling inside, how hard it might be for him to let his father's other children have him when Paulie got so little from him, how all 'in pieces' he might feel as if not being held together any more. She thought about him having missed his session, and so maybe feeling as if he had been forgotten and other children having stolen his time and his counsellor's attention.

As she thought about this and watched, noticing a slightly more solid look to his stance, he picked up some of the toys. They were made to fight in a random, unstructured way. There were no obvious goodies and baddies, with everyone just piling into one another and being thrown to the floor. As she watched she at first felt overwhelmed with the confusion and the chaos, but kept on observing, wondering how much her own feelings were a communication of how he had felt in relation to his family situation. His play began to calm, and slowly more of a narrative emerged, with clearer characters and more shape to the play. He chose out a man doll and a woman doll and made them shout at each other, and then the boy doll pushed them both out of the window. What had been chaotic and randomly destructive was now becoming more of a story, and what is more, a story that she could begin to make sense of, perhaps later to comment on in terms of feelings he was expressing and in a way he could possibly be able to hear.

In the early moments of this session Paulie was far too over-whelmed by his internal chaos to be accessible, and was not really 'playing'. His own inner mess was all there was, with no real possibility of putting any thoughts around it. His body was 'talking' (Parsons and Dermen 1999) as well as his actions, demonstrating how unheld-together he was feeling. However, he was aware of the counsellor watching, and obviously also at some level was aware that she was not herself completely overwhelmed by what was going on in him. She was not coming in with reproaches about his behaviour, nor was she driven to stop him or to make him do something different, she was just watching in this thoughtful way, trying to make sense of what he was doing, and trying to find out what his behaviour was conveying. This in itself helped him begin to structure his thoughts and to approach a state of mind in which some dialogue was possible and some insight into what was going on inside him might emerge.

Being able to observe is the first step towards any intervention, and yet it is surprising how often decisions and judgements are made about a child without their behaviour being properly observed. Observing is not passive; it is an active engagement which is a way of asking a question, and it is sad how often children and adolescents are responded to without anyone stopping to look carefully at how their actions and behaviour relate to what is going on around them. As an example, in one children's home, the attitude of the staff towards their very difficult children was changed radically when they took it in turns to sit out and observe interactions between children and between children and staff. They noticed moments of anxiety and insecurity before anger burst out, they noticed that there was a moment of emotional hurt before a child had a tantrum and realized far more clearly how much of what they had seen as surly intransigence had its roots in the children's emotional vulnerabilities. Observing had enabled a different view of behaviour to emerge, where an emotional story was evident. This enabled them to think about the children and their interactions with them more carefully rather than the problem being conceptualized more as a matter of controls and strategies.

## Putting into words – the running commentary

The second tool that is likely to come into play is the putting into words what is being observed. This is usually much more useful than asking questions about what the child is doing. Thus when

Oladayo (8) walks into the session and falls face downwards into a large cushion, seeming to bury himself in it but saying nothing, it is often going to be more helpful for the counsellor to say something like 'I see that you are burying yourself in the cushion,' than to ask why Oladayo is doing this. If the emphasis in her mind is the way in which he isn't talking to her when normally he might, then she could add 'and maybe not right now wanting to tell me what this is about'. In this way she acknowledges something in him, instead of making it sound as if she needs him to speak. The simple (although not always easy) act of giving the child a thoughtful running commentary can be immensely containing. It is easy to underestimate the power of doing this, as it can seem as if we are not adding anything much. However, just by putting words to what is happening, we are showing that we can take it in, we are not just going to react, and what is more we can think about what the child is showing us. This immediately conveys something important – i.e. that the counsellor is seeing what is being done as significant and as a communication of some kind. We are resisting 'irritably reaching after fact and reason' (Bion 1970, quoting Keats 1817) but are prepared to wait until some meaning comes through. We are also putting words to an action, and this itself gives the action more shape and coherence. We are 'putting a thought bubble' around it, which makes it a shared event. Simple phrases like 'I notice that you …', 'I can see that you …' or 'You want me to see that you …' are very useful, as they shape what is being done, and help the child reflect on their own actions. 'The what has to precede the why' (Alvarez 1992).

Using the example give of Oladayo, above, who plunged into the cushion at the beginning of the session, one could use a number of approaches, depending on the precise nuances of his way of doing it. One might want to say that he seems a bit despairing when he falls into the cushion, if that is what if seems like to the counsellor, or that he seems to want to get right into the cushion and feel safe, escaping the rest of the world, if that is more the sense of it. These are thoughtful guesses that he can take or leave. If we have got it right, he will feel a bit understood and an emotion will have been accepted and validated, but if we have got it wrong he will still hear the attempt to understand and will be alert to our openness to being shown what his real feeling is. Again, the recognition of the feeling needs to come first, before any attempt to think about the 'why'.

In another example, Tamas (7) was making all the toy animals fight each other, with the armies arranged in an orderly way at the beginning but then becoming a riotous tangle with no discernible pattern. We might have many thoughts about this, but if it isn't clear that an interpretation is useful, or if we simply don't yet understand very much, we might just comment on how the armies were clear to begin with, but now it is all a hopeless muddle of fighting, with it not being clear who is on whose side. This is a step towards an appreciation of his own state of mind, but the comment is relatively neutral, so one can gauge by his response how much more he is willing to show us.

Sal (7) was making the mother doll yell at the baby doll, saying it was dirty and smelly, and needed to be punished. We may again have many thoughts about how this connects with Sal's experiences, but often the most useful thing will be to register out loud what we see, perhaps that the mother is really angry, or that she can't stand the baby being dirty and smelly. How Sal responds and what happens next will help us move a little closer to understanding her experience and what she is trying to convey.

A reflective running commentary, coupled with some names for the feelings that seem to be around, is the bedrock of psychodynamic work with younger children, as well as being invaluable in many other approaches and adaptable to many other settings. But in psychodynamic thinking the accurate identifying of what is going on also depends on the work we can do on processing our own responses, thinking about the 'countertransference' (Chapter 2). Regarding Oladayo, in the example above, the counsellor felt curious as to what had happened to make him enter the room this way when he buried himself in the cushion. She felt a bit worried, a bit left out, and made to wait. She could use these feelings, and maybe say something to Oladayo about how he needs her to wait, or wants her to know what it is like to know something is wrong but not know what. Again this is more useful than simply asking him – when and if he wants to explain, he will.

The counsellor therefore observes both with eyes and with the inward eye to her own feelings, so as to be more accurate as to what is being conveyed and stirred up. In the example of Sal, if her counsellor feels shocked and helpless by the mother doll's treatment of the baby, this could be something that can be used in registering to Sal that the counsellor is having to watch the baby being cruelly treated – unable to do anything to stop it. This is still a running commentary, but one which is about the position the counsellor is being put into the frame rather than speaking simply about what the child is doing. This will be more useful than asking Sal for more information, not just because an answer is most likely not to be forthcoming, but because it opens up the interaction as a complex and emotionally dynamic one, between Sal and the counsellor, with the idea that feelings are being registered, observed and commented on. It is likely that the helplessness and shock felt by the counsellor are aspects of the experience that Sal is trying to convey and have processed, so by naming them this process is brought closer to consciousness and becomes more available to thought.

## The interpersonal context

This brings into focus a further key element to this observing, noticing and commenting. The comments, as shown above, convey that there is someone there who is able to take in what the child is doing and how they are feeling. If the comments contain elements like 'You want me to see that …' or 'You want me to know that …' there is another powerful ingredient – the establishing of the behaviour or play in the context of the relationship. There is **interpersonal** significance to what is happening, as well as intrapersonal significance. To clarify, we can use an example of a child picking up the dolls' house parents and hitting them hard onto the floor. At its simplest one might say 'I see you are hitting the mum and dad dolls' or 'those parent dolls are being really bashed'. The next stage would be to say 'It looks like you are angry with the mum and dad dolls'. But one further stage would be to say 'You want **me to see** how angry you are and how much you want to punish the parent dolls'. The latter does not seem to add much, but immediately helps the child understand that what happens in the room is communication to you, not just an explosion. Like with Paulie above, it also conveys the acceptance of the anger, the understanding that anger is a feeling that can be thought about and understood, rather than just condemned.

## Listening

Listening is the next key skill used in psychodynamic work. It sounds a very simple and obvious element, but open-minded and careful listening is not easy. One is listening not just to the words, but to the tone, the kind of language, the coherence or otherwise, the extent that the child is in touch with the feelings behind the words. There may be terrible things being described but in a flat voice. There may be sad things being described with excitement. There may be words or phrases that are repeated, or applied in slightly odd ways. These are always worth attending to, as there will usually be an important unconscious meaning hidden behind the idiosyncrasy and they can provide the clue one needs to decipher an element that cannot be clearly expressed in a more straightforward way. Similarly there may be ways in which the child stops themselves following a train of thought or uses a tone of voice that betrays much more than the words. Moreover there are ways in which the counsellor as listener may be being invited into a particular role. A teenager who comes in and tells you of a long series of times when he has been unfairly treated by the teachers needs you to be listening not only to the facts of his perceived ill-treatment but to the feelings of persecution, and moreover the need for the counsellor to be on his side, to believe his side of the story. This does not mean of course that the counsellor should simply take his side, but it could be helpful to say something about how important it is to him that the counsellor understands how ill-treated he feels.

The questions or responses used to facilitate the listening need to be open, helping the child to say or express more, rather than trying too hard to pin something down. Reflecting back is often useful, as this helps explore rather than narrow the focus. When Maya (8) tells you she is fed up, you can ask why, or you can say 'fed up?' or you can say 'You want me to know you are really fed up'. Or you can wait, and if nothing else comes you can say 'You want me to know you are fed up, but are not sure you want to tell me more'. Direct questions are often the least helpful way to elicit more information, although of course they can still have their place. Often the child needs to know you are listening, and truly attending, if they are to say or show more, and this is often more easily conveyed by a 'running commentary' type response than by a direct request for more information, especially of the 'why' kind. More often than not children will not be able to put into words immediately why they are feeling something or why they did something. Even if they can, they will often give a shallow response based on what they are directly conscious of, which may be far from the real underlying cause. It is better to explore the why together through further attentiveness, and attention to what is not said as well as what is, than to ask for this to be foreclosed with a direct answer.

## Naming feelings

Further to this is the immensely important tool of naming feelings. Examples have already been given of how this can be done in the context of non-verbal play or behaviour showing a range of feelings, but it is a key element in all psychodynamic work, whether the child is working on a verbal level or not. Many children come to us with an inchoate mess of difficult feelings, and many have never experienced an adult who has given these feelings shapes and names. There is so much that can be done simply by helping a child differentiate their feelings more clearly, for example to clarify anger, frustration, fear, despair, sadness, anxiety, hurt and so on. This is partly because feelings do become more manageable when we are more able to focus on them clearly. It is also because by putting words to them, they immediately becomes more 'thinkaboutable' than when what is being experienced is just an urgent but formless surge of something. We also, by naming the feelings, convey that we understand and accept their reality for the child. It is easy to under-estimate, and indeed hard to overestimate, how novel and useful this can be.

Jeanette (14) came in terribly anxious and upset about her sister's Shona's illness. As she spoke it became clear to the counsellor that Jeanette felt that Shona had received more love and attention from her parents as she had always been poorly. Having her jealousy and envy named, with an acknowledgement that she had been really angry when her last birthday party had been ruined by her sister's illness, was a huge relief to her. By knowing she felt angry she could begin to forgive herself for it, and realize that Shona's difficulties were not the result of her wicked jealous wishes. While the feeling remained unnamed and unacknowledged it was much more avail-able to being employed in limitless anxiety. Jeanette had always felt that her jealousy and anger was bad, but the counsellor's calm naming of the feeling brought it into the realm of acceptability and work could begin on integrating it with the love and care she also had for her sister.

## Questions

Questions, although mentioned above as sometimes not being the most useful intervention, are still very much part of the tool box. As already shown, there is a wide range in helpfulness in the kind of questions one could ask. Direct questions with younger children are often unhelpful. The children will for the most part not themselves know in any detail what they are trying to convey, and the uncon-scious content of the play is almost always going to be more impor-tant than what the child thinks the play is about. Therefore it is usually better to comment and let the play unfold, with the possibility that the meaning will become clear if you wait and let the child know you are attending carefully.

With older children or children who are using talk as their primary communication tool there are different ways in which one can try to explore more fully what is being conveyed. It can sometimes be that the most useful kind of question is one of the 'what was that like for you?' or 'where did that leave you?' variety, in order to give the child the opportunity to clarify what their feelings were in the episode being explained. However, this is only likely to work well with children who are already well able to think about their own feelings. With others it is often more useful to say something more like 'I can see that this felt really unfair to you' or 'It sounds as if that really hurt you' rather than 'How did you feel?' The child can correct you if you have imagined wrongly, or might look differently at the feeling they are recollecting in the light of your words, but you might be helping them more by empathically entering into the feeling they are conveying than by just asking.

Where questions can be of the utmost importance is in helping to establish links where the child was not conscious of any. For example, when Siobhan (17) told her counsellor how she had been in a terrible state the evening before, which had led her to self-harm and terrible despair, she had no sense of it having a context. By asking her what had happened just before, it was possible to discover that there had been an ostensibly minor altercation with her sister over the television, which had made Siobhan aware of vivid angry and resentful feelings, which to her were intolerable. As she was unable to stay with her own anger for any time at all, she had turned it into a vicious attack on herself. A careful clarifying of the context of the incident one is being told about can elucidate links that were not evident at first.

Sometimes a question is more of a nudge towards an interpretation, or includes a good deal of insight packaged in a palatable way. For example, Sade (15) was complaining bitterly about how angry her mother was when she came home 'only half an hour late' when 'it's ridiculous that she won't trust me and makes me come home way earlier than all my friends'. Her counsellor asked what it was Sade thought her mother was most worried about happening to her. This was a very ordinary question, but immediately it shifted the emotional energy from defensive fury over perceived control to a sense of the interpersonal reality of parental worry and teenage potential vulnerability. It may or may not be the case that this mother had powerful difficulties in letting her daughter become more independent, but asking about the underlying anxieties and fantasies opened up some space for thinking about this event as a dynamic interaction between the two of them. This then made more room for Sade to try out identifying with her mother and some space to think about the effect on her mother of how she behaved.

In summary, questions do have a place, and can be powerful ways of moving the work on, especially with older children. However, they need to be used sparingly, as in the ways described they are paradoxically less likely to get answers than many other interventions and can foreclose rather than further communication.

# 4

# KEY ELEMENTS OF PSYCHODYNAMIC TECHNIQUE 2

The techniques described in Chapter 3 lend themselves to many settings and can be used to help towards a variety of approaches with children. The tools described in this chapter are more specifically aimed at those working in a more formal and boundaried counselling setting.

## Family trees

One form of questioning which is often invaluable is an enquiry as to the child's family history and relationships. A particularly effective means of asking about this, especially with older children and adolescents, is by making a family tree. This is not something one would do automatically, with every child, as one has to judge whether to do so would intrude unhelpfully on the process of making early contact with the child and/or cut across what it is that they most urgently want to convey. However, it is a tool that has supplied the key to unlocking many cases, and revealed in a swift and economical way links that have made sense of presenting problems and of the way the child is experiencing life.

By doing a family tree one is learning a great deal that is likely to illuminate the story the child is letting you know about. One is also conveying important information by implying that the child's problems are likely to make more sense if seen in the light of the whole family situation, which takes them out of the realm of the child simply being bad or mad. It is far easier for a child to tell you about their family by doing a family tree together than it would be if you just asked. It moves the enquiry from being directly on the child, who may feel uncomfortably in the spotlight, into a mutual effort with the counsellor directed at producing something together. Often the important links are not those that the child would obviously concentrate on if asked more simply. In addition, if there is a vital link, it may be one that the child would unconsciously be defended against revealing, so the tool of the tree can circumvent some defences in an unthreatening and potentially useful and illuminating way.

There are some obvious things that can be explored in doing a family tree. Two of the most important are parental splits and issues around the child's position amongst siblings. In discussing these, one often finds the emotional life of the child becoming clear and accessible. A problem that seemed to be all about feeling left out from school friendships emerges as being closely linked to the preoccupation of mother with a new baby in a new relationship. An issue about failing to get on with preparation for school-leaving exams turns out to have a close relationship with fury with the father who left and who was the one who was most interested in the child's academic progress.

Compiling family trees also often uncovers family life-cycle issues about which the child is not consciously thinking, or whose significance is not being appreciated. For example, one might find out that a grandparent has recently died or that the child in front of you is the last to be at home, with others having already left. One might discover that both parents are immigrants under immense strain as grandparents back home become elderly, with this child carrying the heavy burden of being one of the main reasons the family are in this country. Siblings may have failed or become ill, which has raised great anxieties and increased the pressure on this child to redeem the family. Or siblings may have succeeded all too well, conveying that they cannot be rivalled, so what is there left to achieve? Parents may be isolated or surrounded by extended family; they may be the hope or the shame of their own family. This child may be the only precious child or grandchild, or lost in a huge crowd of others.

It is always useful to ask the parents' ages as well, even if the child does not always know the answer. Sometimes we learn that mother had this child very young, and this puts her anxieties as to her daughter's sexual acting out into a different context, and sheds light on the daughter's own perception of what she is doing. It may reveal that the child was most probably not planned, and give some hints as to the dynamics around the child's arrival in the world. Or we might learn of parents coming to parenthood late, with great anxiety about ever becoming parents, or with miscarriages or other disasters before our client was born, which bring complex family dynamics with them. Sometimes we learn of large differences in age between parents and a sense of Oedipal issues being passed through the generations. We might realize that retirement or menopause are potentially an issue for the parents, and understand more fully what this child stands for as a result. We might find parents who have never fully separated from their own parents, or an opposite story of rifts and irreconcilable differences.

It is also often revealing, especially with adolescents, to ask about the parents' occupations. This can shed useful light on the background of the child, in terms of expectations, the experience of success, failure and inclusion for the parents and the perceived place of the family in the wider world. It can often open up areas of identification or its repudiation between the child and a particular parent, as we learn about their own hopes, likes and dislikes in the context of the family repertoire.

As a way to discover a wide range of vital information, the family tree is an unrivalled resource. Once of its great virtues is its flexibility. We can pause at any stage when we detect an issue emerging that needs further exploration. We can follow the child's own agenda as he or she introduces and describes family members or events. We can ask who else belongs in the picture, including non-family members such as neighbours or family friends, even pets. Most crucially, using it enables us to explore questions that would feel much more intrusive if done as if from a check-list in our mind. How the child gets on with the family members, who is most important to them, how they perceive their identity and place in the family, how they understand the situation the family is in – all these and many more can be explored in a much more organic way than if there was no shared production being made at the time. With younger children we can ask them which colours should be used for each person, which sometimes reveals unconscious links and connections/contrasts that the child would not be able to come up with in words. The children can be actively involved in the work, which engages them in exploring their emotional relationships in their family in a simple but potentially profound way. They might draw the people or write their names using different sizes and positions, which reveal other elements in their view of themselves and their perceptions of their families.

There are many psychodynamic practitioners who would not use this technique, preferring to take up whatever the child presents, and who would not like to do something as proactive and directive as to suggest making a family tree. This is a completely valid point of view, and adheres more strictly to the psychoanalytic model. Also, if one has access to parents and/or has been able otherwise to take a reasonably full history, it is not so necessary. Making family trees, like any other technique, can be used unhelpfully, especially if it is used as an automatic resource and therefore applied indiscriminately. It can be used defensively so as to avoid the crucial immediate encounter with the child or adolescent's distress. However, I have found it invaluable as a resource, and it can be easily harnessed to the larger psychodynamic endeavour (see McGoldrick *et al.* (1999), for a family systems perspective on the use of family trees).

One example was in the work with Christine (16). Her family tree portrayed an immense extended family on both sides. What emerged was a catalogue of disasters: teenage pregnancies, mental illness, suicide, drug abuse and alcoholism. The family was also riven with feuds, with this part of the family not talking to that part. Relationships broke and could not be repaired, people fell and could not be rescued. It shed an invaluable light on her behaviour in school, in which she acted tough and denied the need for any connections with others, apart from those founded on fear. When looked at in the light of her family experience, it was not surprising that vulnerability and neediness were extraordinarily risky. This did not mean that her problems were seen as less serious, as they were self-destructive and significantly impeding her development. What it did do was transform my view of her. Instead of seeing her as someone making rather a mess of being 16, I could begin to appreciate what an achievement it was that she had got this far without falling off the rails completely, and to see that she deserved great respect for being able to come to counselling at all. This enabled a greater focus on her resources and capacity to manage herself rather than on what was destructive in her. She herself was taken aback by the overall picture, and also managed to see that she was not doing so badly after all. Her own idea about her place in the world began to shift.

There is further discussion of the use of family trees, in Chapter 14 on short-term work, as they are often the core of a therapeutic consultation. They need to be used with care but can be hugely useful in both short- and long-term work.

## Interpretation

Interpretation is often seen as the powerhouse of psychodynamic work. The archetypal classical full-scale psychoanalytic interpretation (Strachey 1933) is one that links infantile experience to the present day, puts into words how the transference relationship is linked to the client's early life, and explains how the unconscious forces at work in the client's experience of the therapist are influencing his present-day relationships with himself and others. The occasions on which one can use this kind of interpretation, however, are rare enough in full psychoanalytic work, and it is debatable whether this is in reality the keystone of the work, particularly with children in less intensive settings.

The kind of comments I have outlined in earlier sections on technique are powerful interventions in their own right, despite not being strictly speaking interpretations. The working through in the counter-transference and transference (Joseph 1985; O'Shaughnessy 1992) of the dynamics that dominate the child's life is done through the emotional encounter in the room being taken in, processed, made sense of and finally commented on by the counsellor. Even when the commenting stage is not explicitly reached, a great deal goes on that is useful to the child, as the counsellor struggles to clarify for herself what the child is experiencing, what the counsellor is being invited to experience, and then what sense can be made of this in the child's overall emotional world. The counsellor can interpret this to the child as and when it is clear enough what is happening, with due attention to the age and level of understanding of the child, but even if she does not, the way in which her understanding informs her way of relating to the client will convey her message in ways that words sometimes would not.

Often the work is more explicitly done through a different kind of interpretation, that of clarifying the dynamics of relationships presented to the counsellor and of identifying the inner conflicts that are causing the problems for the child. Patterns will emerge in the stories they tell, the games they play or the drawings they make and these will lead to an understanding of the child's experience of the outside world and illuminate their internal world. This can be interpreted in a way that helps the child understand themselves more fully.

For example, Peter (14) came in full of grievance against the unfairness of his parents' restrictions on his life, and describing the things he was doing that brought about his being grounded. These included a number of risky behaviours in which he had come close to getting into serious trouble. It became clear to me that Peter was himself anxious and nervous about the dangers he was flirting with, but was denying this in order to pretend to himself that he was fearless and powerful. He was projecting all his anxiety into his parents and despising their vulnerability and fear, leaving himself free to nurse his sense of injustice at being restricted. Once I made it possible for him to allow for his own fears and concerns, what looked like a simple inter-personal conflict became more clearly visible as intrapersonal – the tussle inside Peter between his adolescent omnipotence and his vulnerability. This was more painful for Peter than having rows with his parents, but was much more likely to lead to him taking better care of himself and being able to stop his own headlong rush into defiant self-destructiveness.

Often what the child is talking about or showing us is a demonstration of how old or fundamental conflicts are being replayed in current life. The wrangles with teachers or the upheavals in friendships are getting some of their power and becoming intractable because they have connections with or roots in much deeper and more serious troubles that the child has encountered. For example, Yemi (13) told me that he was suspicious when a classmate was nice to him, and then had his fears confirmed when he ended up doing all the work on a shared project. He was being taken advantage of. The fear that this was going to happen made him suspicious whenever anyone was nice to him. It was not hard to spot the parallels here with his home life. Yemi's mother had been ill for a long time, and he had to do a great deal as her carer. To him, his experience of being loved was painfully bound up with having to do a lot to please and care for his parent, with little felt experience of having a parent look after him. His anger and sense of grievance about this made him doubt the nature of affection, and really not securely know how to tell the difference between someone who liked him and someone who wanted a service from him. He was worried that this might make him lose the chance of a real friendship. Elucidating this with him helped him see how he was bringing unacknowledged issues from home into school, which were interfering with his social interactions.

Another typical kind of interpretation might be used when what looks like a narrow current conflict is shown to connect with something denied or forgotten from long ago. Take Greta (16), who had missed large chunks of school and was in danger of losing out seriously as public exams loomed on the horizon. She hated school because she feared being asked questions to which she didn't know the answers. This had started in primary school when she was diagnosed with a learning difficulty and felt that the teachers just wanted to get rid of her. She felt rejected and humiliated by their behaviour towards her. In exploring her history it emerged that her father had stopped contact visits at around the same time as her diagnosis. When she first spoke of this she said that she had forgotten all about him, and didn't care about the stopping of the visits. When I clarified her emotions around school – hurt, humiliation, rejection and a feeling of not being wanted, I said it was striking how much these sounded like how she might have reacted when her father ceased contact with her. She started to cry and tearfully told me that she had told her mother she didn't mind, but she **had** minded. She had tried to put it out of her mind and had managed to forget. She could see that the power the fear of rejection and humiliation had over her was importantly driven by the buried feelings about her father.

The following week Greta came back, having spent every day in school and having talked at length to her mother. She said it made sense that 'it had all been about Dad'. She felt quite different now, and didn't think she would miss any more school. She had woken up each day wanting to come and was already feeling the benefit of not being so behind.

As a tool, interpretation needs to be handled with care. Interpretations and insight can be used aggressively (Dyke 1987). An example of this might be if we point out how a child acting so tough is doing so because inside they feel small and vulnerable. This may be in one sense true but can be said in retaliation to belittle and be like prodding a child on their sorest spot. Or interpretation can be using an inappropriate 'grammar' (Alvarez 1997), which ignores the state of mind of the child and ends up making the child feel worse. Wording can be crucial. For example, following Alvarez' teaching, it is often much better to speak about it being difficult to believe something good than to speak about a fear of something bad. For example, it is usually better to say to a child that it is 'hard for you to believe that I will keep coming back to see you' rather than 'you are afraid that I might not come back'. It is better to say that you 'find it hard to hope that this horrible situation might change' rather than 'you are afraid that this is how things will always be'. Such issues of wording might seem small at first sight, but they can make a big impact on how the child hears us. The emphasis on the fear may confirm and exacerbate their anxieties, while emphasizing the difficulty in grasping the better alternative makes it that bit more potentially available. We can think it, so maybe they can glimpse it too.

There is not space in this book to go into all the subtleties of interpretation (see Sternberg 2005 for an excellent brief introduction to the subject), but any psychodynamic practitioner needs to be aware that, as with anything that is potentially powerful for great good, interpretation can also be used badly and can either cause the child to close down communication or increase their distress.

However, a sensitively worded and timed interpretation, in the context of an emotional connection between the client and the counsellor, can be of profound importance and can bring about both an emotional experience for the child that is deep and lasting – that of being understood – and a sense of something unconscious being grasped cognitively in his mind. What matters is that the interpretation increases the experience of genuine contact between the counsellor and the client, around a piece of genuine new understanding, and this can only come if both empathy and intellect are at work. Intellectual insight on its own is not helpful as it can feel like the 'application of technique', which will not bring about a 'moment of meeting' (Stern *et al.* 1998).

## Working with and working in transference and countertransference

As described in Chapter 2 on key elements of psychodynamic theory, one of the most distinctive and important characteristics of psychodynamic work is the prominence given to understanding and working with the transference and the countertransference. In this section I will outline some ways in which this can be used in practice.

### *Transference*

It is a fundamental tenet of the psychodynamic approach that the child recreates in the room with the counsellor elements of their inner world of relationships. As part of this, we in our role as counsellor will be experienced in ways that are powerfully derived from other, earlier relationships. The child is unaware of this, as their experience is, to them, simply what is real, but we are in a privileged position to monitor who we appear to be in the child's perception. We can gauge how we are being experienced, and this gives us a direct piece of evidence as to the unconscious workings of the child's mind.

Most often there is evidence that we are being experienced in a way familiar from descriptions of other people in a child's life. As a simple example, a child may tell us that the teachers are always making fun of her and seeing her as stupid. It will be important in a situation like this to watch out for and to alert her to moments when she is expecting this to be happening in the room with us, or that she will find it hard to believe that we too won't see her this way. She may work hard to make a split between us and the rest of the world, in which we are the only one who doesn't treat her this way. Splitting the world into good and bad, idealizing some people while denigrating others, is a typical way of defending oneself, trying to cope with the messy reality of relationships with people about whom we have mixed feelings. If we go along with this split and allow the idealization, we forgo an important possibility of working to help the child make sense of what is going on and to integrate some contemptuous and/or despised aspects of herself.

Aliya (15) was always fearful that she was resented, taking up space in the family that was really someone else's. She felt that everyone would be better off without her. It was useful in this case not to leave that as an outside event, but to ask her how that worked here between her and me. She thought about this, and realized that she did feel that there were many other children in the school who deserved a counselling session more than her, and that if she were not coming I could get on with much more rewarding and useful work. This helped her see how pervasive the pattern was and gave us a direct route into the dynamics she was describing.

More difficult is when a transference is being experienced and acted on by the child but not explicitly talked about either in the here-and-now or in relationships outside. So a child who is overly careful about mess or is placatory in their play or manner may be experiencing us as a critical or fragile parent. In a different case we may become aware that the child is relating to us as a playmate who is the same age rather than as an adult in a position of some power. By careful attention to how he behaves and deals with our presence, we can piece together who we are in his mind, at this particular time. I add that last comment as, of course, this can change from session to session and indeed from moment to moment. But how they relate to us and how this changes is a direct route into understanding the nature of the figures and relationships in their inner world.

As this section is on technique, the key issue here needs to be what to do with transference when we identify it. The first thing we can and will do, simply by virtue of our understanding of its nature and whether or not we feel able to offer interpretations, is to react differently from the way we would if we thought that the child was responding simply to how we are ourselves. Even if we do not comment on the transference, we can avoid reactions that would either confirm the child's projections or attempt to prove to them that we are not the way they are seeing us. If the child is coming to the sessions in a way that shows they see us as stupid and useless, it is vital that we accept that projection and process it, rather than retaliate or try to prove otherwise. If we can bear the projection, without masochistically accepting it, we have a foothold on understanding it and ultimately being able to work with it.

Once we have seen what is going on in the transference and have avoided being acted on by it directly, we can then explore it, helping the child to notice it and to become aware of how they are seeing us, with some thought available that this may not be the simple truth. Just by commenting on how they are seeing us can be enough for it to become possible for them to become curious about this, and to become more aware that they are at the least in part co-creating that impression. This is the first step towards the gradual lessening in the power of the projection, and can be part of engendering that vital curiosity about their own thought processes and emotional responses that will enhance the work.

## Countertransference

Recognizing, understanding and working with the countertransference is one of the most distinctive and crucial aspects of psychodynamic work, and can always be of use, whether interpretation is indicated or not. It is a tool that every psychodynamic counsellor has to learn to use if they are to be worthy of the name – and any other practitioner will be helped in their work by having an understanding of it. If we can process how we are being made to feel by the child or adolescent in front of us, we are immediately in possession of a powerful array of technical possibilities that can help us enormously both in managing ourselves and in helping the client. One of the most important aspects of understanding the countertransference is in helping us cope with the impact on us of the children's disturbance. It helps us think about experiences and feelings that for them are not think-about-able. However, as well as the unspoken processing that is so fundamental in psychodynamic work, there is more that one can do with the countertransference to make it available for thinking in the room.

For example, Lee, a 9-year-old boy, makes his counsellor feel very stupid. She cannot think and she feels useless. He treats her with contempt and sneers at everything she does. He rampages around the room and she feels powerless. In such a scenario, the counsellor first has to register that her feeling of uselessness and stupidity is a countertransference, which can be hard, particularly as a beginner may be only too easily made to feel that she is out of her depth and should never have tried to become a counsellor in the first place. But if she can step back and give herself the mental space to process the feeling and recognize it as countertransference, there is a range of options open to her.

At one end of the spectrum, if she is unable to manage and process her own feelings and just pushes them back at him, she might say that he is acting like this because he must himself be feeling stupid and useless. This kind of interpretation may not be factually wrong but it is very unlikely to be helpful and is not to be recommended, as it is often an aggressive use of insight, designed to push back the bad feeling into the child so as not to have to bear it oneself. At the other extreme she could just hold onto the feeling and not say anything, but think about it and try to understand it. Next to this would be a verbal recognition of the way he is feeling about it, for example, 'You clearly feel I am stupid and useless to you today'. This shows she can think about these horrible feelings rather than act on them or project them. It also shows she can accept that this is how he feels. The use of the word 'today' helps him register that this may not be how he always feels, and that she knows this. It puts some thought around the interaction between them, and creates a space where the feelings in the room can be reflected on. Next along the spectrum might be something like 'it seems as if I am to feel useless and stupid today', or 'you want me to know how useless and stupid I am in your eyes'. This makes it a bit more obvious that he is doing this to you, although it is only suggested. Then might come, if she thinks the child can manage it, 'It seems as if I am the one who has to feel useless and stupid today. Maybe that is so I can know how you feel sometimes', or 'you want me to know what it's like to feel useless and stupid, because you want me to understand how awful that can be for you.'

Thus the countertransference can be simply processed and borne, fed back as the child's perception or interpreted as the child's projected feelings, with degrees of directness depending on what the child can process and, of course, the shared vocabulary of the work already established. Each child will teach us what they can make use of, and we need to take the work at a pace the child can manage.

It is worth noting that it takes time, experience and confidence to be able to recognize, understand and use both transference and countertransference. It can be difficult for us when starting out to be able to discern the transference elements in how we are being seen and reacted to, as opposed to taking the child's response to us as being a result of our actual presentation and ability. It is also important to pay attention to how we present ourselves so we can be alert to how much is the child's production and how much we are bringing it about (Chapter 7). It can be hard, without the confidence born of long experience, to sort out how much what we are feeling is our own, and how much is the result of the child's projective identification. This is one of many reasons why good supervision is essential for anyone working in this way, especially and most acutely early on but also throughout our career as a counsellor. We need the perception and skill of an experienced supervisor to help us discern and disentangle the different elements that go into the dynamics between us and the child. In order to remain able to process the impact on us of the child's emotional reality and the invitations to become part of their inner world, we need someone who can look at the interaction from the outside. They will help us work out how we are feeling and why, as well as how the child is feeling and why. As a result we will become more receptive and perceptive, and develop the ability to use our own emotional reactions more accurately as a guide to the psychic reality of our clients (Wilson 2003; Omand 2009).

## Working in the metaphor

There are many situations when working explicitly in the transference and countertransference feels as if it would be more than the child can manage, and/or might cut across self-expression through play or behaviour, preventing more from emerging. It is often helpful to 'stay in the metaphor', to use a phrase from play therapy. This means using all the techniques described above regarding the running commentary and the naming of feelings, but keeping this in relation to, for example, the dolls or animals. Emotional scenarios and interactions can be explored and understood, relationships described and emotional stories played out, without explicit links to the child's own experience. The emphasis may be on how frightened the little pig is, how hard it is for him when there doesn't seem to be anyone there to help him, how much he needs to be superstrong and fierce to keep the wolf away and never let on that he might be frightened, etc., without the links to the child's own fear and defensive structure being brought out. With some children this works very well indeed, with the emotional nature of the stories changing as the child clarifies and explores their inner world in the context of a thoughtful and insightful commentator. There can be great change worked through the child's own self-healing in this facilitating context (Chapter 7) and it is not always necessary to put into words how you see this connecting to the transference or to the child's own life. As the work progresses, making the connections explicit may become more possible but it is by no means always needed, and can be actively unhelpful if done too early and/or forcefully.

## Interpretations and reality

It is often not helpful to be too specific and explicit about the home situation we think the child is referring to in their play. Linking interpretative comments too closely to actual relationships can both miss the mark and sometimes even make things worse. This is partly because we may well not be right, and being so specific may lose us some connectedness with the child. Even if we are in one sense right about what is being portrayed, it may not be emotionally manageable for the child to think about it consciously, and to have what is symbolic rendered actual. It is also implying that there is a direct relationship between the play and external reality, when the focus that is usually going to be most helpful to the child is on their internal worlds. It is the child's inner world that is being portrayed in the play; it will have some relationship to the outer world but not a simple one, and we will usually not know what it is. It is generally far more useful to take up the emotional 'shape' of the play, to clarify and interpret the relationships involved and the emotional interplay than simplistically to link this directly to what goes/went on with Mum, Dad, brother, etc. If we too readily take up inner world communications as direct comments on their relationships at home, it can actually exacerbate tensions at home, create loyalty conflicts and invite splitting.

Whatever we choose to say or not say, we will always be watching play or listening to what they tell us without knowing how much or how closely it is based on reality. This is true whatever the age group and is also a factor with adolescents who talk rather than play about their lives. A typical example would be Krishini (15), who spoke in the first session about what came over as an appalling and irretrievably damaged relationship with her mother. She described a chronicle of cruelty and rejection over most of her life. In the following one or two sessions, through gentle exploration and inter- pretation of her own conflicts, the pressure to be understood was relieved to some extent, and she was helped to recognize her own anxiety, desperation and rage. What appeared solely a conflict with her mother hid many internal struggles that were overwhelming her. She then spoke about her mother in a way that was completely unrecognizable, showing her to be offering a far more positive contribution to Krishini's life. Krishini apparently did not notice the degree of contrast in her accounts. A better inner world leads to improvements in external relationships, but it also gives us access to better elements already existing in our relationships that we had been ignoring, denying or unable to access.

There are, as ever, exceptions to the idea that we should not directly link what we see to relationships in the real world. We must never ignore the fact that the child might be telling us about their real emotions in relation to real events and sometimes, with care, an explicit link does need to be made if the child is to feel understood. Children can portray scenes from home or class life that alarm us. They may show things happening to doll children or toy animals that make us fear for their safety. We know that they may be putting into their play all their own passion and fury, their own wish for violent retribution, their own often starkly black and white world, where splitting is a key way of avoiding internal conflict (Klein 1946), and we need to bear in mind that what is going on at home may not be anything like so bleak. However, it may be that the child is actually trying to let us know about something that seriously needs attention, but which cannot yet be spoken about. If a child is using their play to alert us to the possibility of real abuse, then of course it is essential that we are in a position to pick this up. This can be, for some children, the only way they can let adults know about abusive situations (Sinason 1988a) and it is incumbent upon us to be alert to this kind of message. There will be times when the child communicates to us that they are being or have been abused and we will then need to pass on to others our concerns and consider invoking safeguarding procedures.

On a less serious note, but still worth remembering, if the child is ready to see parallels with their own life it can be important to make them explicit, and sometimes insulting to them if you don't. As an example, Charlie (6), who shared out his time painfully between his separated mother and father, was playing a violent game of catch with me using a toy rabbit. He supplied a running commentary on the rabbit's being dropped or flung violently between us. When I spoke gently about the rabbit's emotions in relation to this, he said scornfully, 'This **is** me you know!'

This completes the section on psychodynamic techniques. The following chapters will outline many more examples of how the approach can be used in particular situations, but underlying all the interventions the practitioner will be using some combination of the tools described, even if also marrying them to other approaches or adapting them to other settings.

# 5

# THE DEVELOPMENTAL PERSPECTIVE

Anyone working with children and adolescents needs to have a strong sense of the developmental perspective in their work with their clients. By this I mean that it is crucial that the child's presentation is understood in the context of a grasp of the particular features, challenges and tasks of their age group. How we understand a child and how we assess their ways of functioning has to be closely connected to their developmental stage, and if we are to see what is going badly or well for them we need to have a sense of where their development is progressing as expected and where it may be blocked or slow, or indeed precocious and premature. We also need to have a sense of what their key underlying preoccupations are likely to be at different ages, so that we can better tune in to how they are managing the transitions inherent in growing up.

Often what one does as a child or adolescent counsellor is endeavour to clear away obstacles to the normal developmental processes, which for one reason or another have become stalled or stuck. Moving on to the next stage of life may be rendered impossible by the level of anxiety aroused, or by the way in which it has not yet been possible for the child to master the challenges of the earlier stage. There may be a real or perceived absence of the emotional and other resources required to move on and to take the next steps in growing up. Counselling can be a way of helping the child or adolescent to reorganize their internal landscape in such a way that the developmental drive has a clearer path into the future.

As mentioned above, while some children may appear stalled in their development, in contrast one can meet children (or more familiarly adolescents) who are trying to jump right over stages of growing up and transforming themselves into instant adults.

Perhaps as a result of being so anxious about the challenges of the stage ahead they defend themselves by trying to deny any need to learn or grow and instead accelerate into pseudo-maturity.

Therefore to assess a child and understand where, how and to what extent problems have arisen, the developmental perspective is a key ingredient. In addition, each stage of development will naturally be posing its own challenges, and bringing into focus its own imperatives. Daniel Stern has introduced the term 'clinical windows' – that is moments during stages of development when particular issues come to the fore in a form that can be most readily worked with and influenced (Stern 1995). If we are attuned to these we can focus the work more accurately on the issues most at stake, and be able to choose an emphasis that most reflects the developmental challenges faced by the child in front of us.

## Early years

While child and adolescent counsellors might indeed be involved with families with very young children, it is likely that for most the youngest clients coming their way will be at the beginning of a child's school life. Therefore, even though the psychodynamic approach can be invaluable in work with babies and toddlers it is beyond the scope of this book to look in any detail at infant development. (See Baradon *et al.* 2005 and Pozzi 2007, for application of psychodynamic thinking to this age group, and Waddell 1997, for an overview of emotional development during the early years.)

At the start of a child's school career, from the child's viewpoint there are all the fears and excitements of separation; 'Is it all right to leave the security of home?' – 'Is it all right for you?' and even if it is, 'Is it all right for Mum?' Will she remember to come at the end of the day and find you again? Even for those who are used to nursery care for whom separation is not such an issue, starting school is still a major milestone and is felt to be a marker of a significant move onwards and outwards. It marks a stage in the child's but also the family's life-cycle that can arouse painful and difficult feelings. It involves a widening of the child's circle to include many more adults and children, and brings a focus outside the home that will take up much more of the child's emotional and physical attention.

For all children the issues are powerful. Even those from secure and loving homes are going to find starting school a challenge. How do you manage all those other children and a teacher who is often too busy or distant to notice you? How do you make sense of the bewildering size and complexity of the building and all the new rules and expectations, some explicit but many more just the way things are done that you have to somehow pick up as you go along? How do you cope with suddenly having to compete with so many other 'siblings', not only for attention and support, but also regarding learning and achieving? It is always hard to manage all this, and of course it is especially difficult if you have not had the chance to settle securely in yourself who you are, which is always likely to be the case for children this young. A fragile sense of self can make the melée of school very threatening. Often children come to school with a personality far from consolidated, and sometimes with little equipment developed to manage their feelings or to feel able to hold onto their own emotional responses rather than act them out. They need help in beginning to be able to think about themselves, and to have words or ideas about feelings. At this stage children are often experiencing and expressing their emotional states in concrete ways, with little symbolization. They have stomach aches instead of worries, and need suddenly to go to the toilet instead of being able to speak about their difficult feelings. They may find transitions difficult, as they fear disintegration and being lost and cannot rely on memory and thought to hold onto or feel held on to by others.

Envies and jealousies about depending on and sharing both mother and teacher can be overwhelming. Other children can seem like the enemy and school can feel like a place of terror. Infantile anxieties and defences, only recently experienced and partially overcome for the first time, can be powerfully re-aroused by all this. The children's capacity to hold themselves together is precarious and chaos and confusion can be close at hand. It can be hard through all of this to keep an avenue open for new relationships and the possibility of learning. As well as the demands of school, family stresses are continually impinging on all children, when they have little equipment with which to process and think about them. As the children's worlds widen the possibility is greatly increased that there will be a clash between the defences established in their earliest years, to deal with these stresses, and the new demands and expectations of the outside world, leading to the children becoming identified as having or being a problem.

Later, the anxiety might be around friendships and negotiating life with less support during the primary years. For all the vaunted calm of the 'latency' stage between early childhood and adolescence (Freud 1905), it is well-recognized that it is a time of great pressure and vulnerability (Waddell 1997), and the need for order and stability in the cause of building up a solid sense of self is often not met. There can be massive anxiety over one's place in the world, the integrity of the home and over how much one is liked and how much one is loved. Passionate jealousies and worries about success or failure are strong during this time, even if sexuality *per se* is not yet fully on the agenda. Many children are only just beginning to be able to be thoughtfully aware of their own family story and their own history, and during latency a lot of working out of all this needs to be done. It is a time when one might become much more aware that other families have different stories. For those with troubled, broken or reconstituted families, there is a powerful piece of processing that has to be done if the child is to make good use of this time.

The predominant style of their relationships both with their peer group and with authority figures is established during this period. Vicious circles in these relationships can easily get set up which are hard to break. One has to find one's place in the group, to manage the dynamics of group life, cope with being alike or different, being teased or tempted to bully, grapple with one's academic abilities and limitations, cope with being criticized and challenged, being told what to do and how to behave. A lot can go wrong, and if it is not addressed in these years, then the stage is set for a turbulent and possibly destructive adolescence.

Latency is often characterized by a desire for order, fierce splitting between good and bad, and a need for conformity (Wilson 1989). The collecting, labelling, organizing and accumulation of comprehensive knowledge about one area of activity (cars, football teams, dinosaurs, etc.) are the typical manoeuvres of this age group. All of these are potentially healthy aspects of an ordinary latency, but all can be exaggerated and become counter-developmental. The normal thoughtlessness and clannishness of childhood can be exaggerated into sadistic cruelty, and the need for order can become an obsessional difficulty with change or lack of control. Learning about a limited area of fact-based knowledge can crowd out the need to learn more flexibly, and thinking can become rigid and devoid of meaning. The child now has a body strong enough to do real harm, even if still limited, and this means having to manage impulses that could be more potentially dangerous. These impulses can either threaten to – or actually – get out of control, or they can be over-controlled at the expense of relatedness or the capacity to learn (Chapter 6). Either extreme can become an established way of functioning during this period that can be hard for the child to change.

Negotiating the latency period sets the scene for the next huge upheaval when childhood gets left behind and the child has to move on via puberty into adolescence. If latency has been a troubled time, then it is highly unlikely that adolescence will be encountered without major difficulty, but in addition, some children who have apparently managed latency with relative ease can come unstuck in their teens.

## Puberty and adolescence

Puberty is a particularly stressful and complex time for children, particularly when emotional and physical development is out of synch. It is not uncommon to come across adolescents who have adult-like bodies while inside there is still quite a small child struggling reluctantly with new feelings and urges and the different reactions and expectations from others. There can be a great fear about joining the adult sexual world, and a great need to hang on to childhood. It can be overlooked just how much has to be mourned of one's childhood for it to be possible to move into adolescence (Noonan 1983; Waddell 1998). Children who are frightened of or defying some aspect of school or social life are often caught up in a grave anxiety about growing up. It is frequently the case that this emerges around transition to secondary school. For example, Trisha (11) was bitterly angry about being sent to her secondary school, when she wanted to go to another one. She was utterly miserable in school, and told her counsellor repeatedly about how much she hated it and how much she wanted to leave.

Ostensibly it appeared that this was about other friends going to the other school, and about some of the particular features of the current school. These were real concerns, but behind and beneath them was another deeply felt anxiety and grievance, that she had not been able to stay at primary school and stay a child. Her intense conflicts about this were being disguised as a protest about the choice of school. This served to distract both her and the adults around her from a much more painful area, which was around her great difficulty in taking on board that her own growing up was unstoppable and not under her control.

But one can also find the opposite. Jeremy (12) presented as a cherubic little boy. He was referred by his parents because he had become obsessively curious/anxious about what his parents were up to in their bedroom following inadvertently seeing pornographic imagery on a friend's computer. When encouraged to talk more generally about himself, amongst other things he let me know about a difficult time two years ago when he had been in a lot of trouble, worrying his mother with his naughtiness. From the referral it looked as if he was struggling with the way in which his thoughts about and his relationship with his parents had changed because of the distressing image from the film. However, from the story of his earlier difficult period it became rapidly clear that this was cloaking another more serious anxiety, that his image as a charming little boy would soon be contaminated by the much angrier and more aggressive feelings that were struggling to find expression. We discovered that the disturbing sexual image dominated his mind when he was angry, and it appeared to be a way of attacking his much-loved parents in his mind. Once we had sorted this out, the problem abated rapidly and he did not need to see me any more. So a problem that looked so much as if it had to do with difficulty in facing his sexual parents and his own sexual future turned out to be much more about his growing independence and the aggression that went with it, which he feared would damage his relationship with his parents, particularly his mother.

Another child Raquel (12) was more typical in that she was pretending to be far more invulnerable and sophisticated than she was. She presented as much older, and was embroiled in a chronic confrontation with her parents, particularly her father. She was, from the stories I heard, supremely provocative and unreachable, always indignant as she 'hadn't done anything wrong' and always refusing to talk to them if they tried to approach her. In the first session I discovered that she had been a scared little girl until about a year ago. Puberty hit, and with it a desperate wish to leave that scared little girl behind. She sensed a whiff of her adolescent power, and suddenly discovered that she could scare others, including her parents. She swiftly opted for being one of the tough girls, and had left all the adults around her gasping in shock. Underneath the tough exterior there was a girl who, we discovered, had felt that she lost her loved father when his own mother died, and who felt that she lost her loved mother when her baby brother was born. She could not bear how sad, bereft and frightened she was. All her fears about growing up were being projected (Klein 1946) into the adults, as she put herself increasingly at risk and rejected all attempts to protect her.

## Mid-adolescence

Even if some of these early adolescent challenges have been met successfully, the next hurdles to face are the risks of failure and anxieties around success as public exams are approached. This is when the young person really has to take on board that they have responsibility for their futures, and this often evokes panic. It is the time when their own capacities, both in terms of intellect and in terms of self-discipline, will be sorely tried but it is so much more than that. It, like so many of the new freedoms of adolescence, puts them directly in touch with their propensity to be either self-nurturing or self-destructive, with new real power to affect the trajectory of their lives.

This is a stage perfectly set for acting out, not only in the sense of unhelpful defences against anxiety, but also in the sense of having a new and uniquely powerful arena for enacting difficulties with their parents. Many 16 year olds coming up to public examinations with whom I have worked have been in part paralysed in their attempts to study effectively for exams by their fury and sense of grievance towards their parents. To do well felt like allowing the parents off the hook for all their real and fantasized failures. At last life has handed the youngsters a powerful weapon that really feels as if it works: their own future. Adolescence is full of opportunities to do damage to this future; drugs, sexual acting out and academic failure all beckon with great seductiveness – both as ways of dealing with or avoiding dealing with anxieties, but also as ways of using one's own self, the parents' precious production, as the supreme weapon.

For some adolescents with whom I have worked, a related but different problem presents itself in that they are doing better than their parents did, many of whom left school with no qualifications at all. These young people are often unconsciously deeply worried about overtaking their parents, and unsure if they are 'allowed'. They get mixed messages from home, great pressure to succeed with an undercurrent of envy and depression in the parents as they re-encounter their own failures at school. Ambition for us all is potentially creative and productive but is also full of the unconscious desire to triumph over the parents (Freud 1916), and for some this provokes such anxiety that they are tempted to give up instead.

Teenagers coming up to public exams are likely to be experiencing a crash course in facing reality. For some this reality might be that they have a real chance of major success. For those for whom self-denigration has been a mainstay of their self-image and a defence against having to make an effort, this is a huge responsibility and a challenge. Others will have to relinquish some cherished fantasies about themselves and start to become adjusted to their limitations. Perhaps for the first time they have genuinely to face the reality of the possibilities of their futures and begin truly to understand the consequences of their actions. This can be painful, as true responsibility for oneself and one's actions has to be taken on board. In Kleinian terms one is being asked to make a fuller transition into the depressive position (Klein 1940), where one has to face one's capacity to damage, to manage loss, regret and remorse. For some this is too difficult, and a regression away from the challenge ensues. Self-sabotage in the lead-up to major examinations can often have its roots in such dynamics.

## Later adolescence

There is then the area of particular difficulty, in mid- and later adolescence, relating to the upheavals, uncertainties and risks of the beginnings of the young people's sexual lives. Sex can be used both as an aid to or an avoidance of intimacy. Sexual encounters can be sought as a desperate need for reassurance that one is wanted, as well as being desired for their own sake. The pursuit of excitement can be employed effectively as a defence against and denial of underlying depression. Becoming a sexual being is something that no-one finds easy, and the painful, difficult process of discovering and becoming more at ease with one's sexuality, whatever it may be, is fraught with pitfalls. The pressure to become sexual is strong much earlier now, and this can be hard for many young people to deal with. They not only have their own mind-blowing encounters with sexual desire to manage, but also the confusions engendered by the expectations and rivalries with others, who will mostly be making it look as if they are finding it all much easier. Sexual activity can become a highly fraught arena for competitiveness, both literal (i.e. competing for a particular partner) but also more general (i.e. who has the most success with the opposite sex or is seen as the most desirable) and, as we know only too well, is a most fertile ground for terribly hurtful bullying and humiliation around attractiveness and sexuality. What is already a highly anxious time is made so much more so by the way in which adolescents so often transform their own vulnerability into a need to make others feel insecure and persecuted with thoughts of unlovability. It is an area where unconscious forces can be at their most powerful, with the capacity to make good choices under siege from every side.

It is a commonplace that adolescents are struggling with issues of dependence and independence, but it is a commonplace because it is such a universal and problematic issue. Taking charge of oneself is a task that has to be undertaken, but it is a double-edged experience, with the rewards and excitements of freedom set against the anxieties and burdens of self-reliance. Within the adolescent the yearning to be loved and looked after fights with the need to separate and to break free of parental control. One can feel so invulnerable and omnipotent at this age, immortal even, so parental restrictions can seem petty and just to do with control. One needs gradually to take up the reins of one's own life, but there is rarely a smooth transition from parental controls to self-control! Splitting and projective mechanisms are particularly powerful at this stage, offering ways of compartmentalizing one's experience and offloading anxieties and insecurities into others. Everything can be experienced in such extremes, with unprecedented degrees of elation and excitement being succeeded in short order by desperate vulnerability, misery and/or self-hatred.

## Self-destructiveness and risk

I have already written about academic self-destructiveness, but in adolescence there is also a great potential to turn one's increasing capacity to do harm onto oneself. Our gradual, often painful establishment of our identity is almost always accompanied by moments of extreme self-loathing, as well as perhaps moments of manic elation and grandiosity in which we are going to conquer the world. Despair and depression are commonly encountered when we try to negotiate both our potential and our limitations. It can be hard for us to see a way forward, and for many adolescents the difficulty in facing their own emotional conflicts, anxiety, anger and disappointment can be so great that they turn on themselves either by self-harm, suicidal thoughts or even suicidal actions. This is not the place to go into detail as to the causes of such activities, nor how one would deal with them in counselling (Turp 2006; Heyno 2009). However, working with adolescents requires us to have a good knowledge of these dynamics, to be alert to the signs of and potential for this kind of serious and dangerous acting out and to understand the sources and power of self-destructiveness.

It is important but difficult when assessing adolescents to allow for the melodramatic way they can present themselves and for the swings from apparently suicidal depression to manic triumph without either overreacting or missing crucial signs of something very serious indeed. Maryam (15) had been immersed in a depression that included visits to websites describing suicidal methods. She was attending regularly and seemed slowly to be emerging from the worst of this, when suddenly in one session she began laughing uncontrollably at a memory of the way another girl had looked when she had fallen down. It was unnerving and concerning, and over the next few sessions a similar oscillation was repeated. I was considering whether she was in danger of becoming seriously ill, when she began to settle more and develop a greater capacity to be free of depression without fleeing into manic triumph. What I had been witnessing was a transitory phase, rather than deep-rooted pathology, and with adolescents one has to be alert to the instability of mood that characterizes this stage of development.

This example illustrates how important it is diagnostically to be constantly aware of the nuances of the different developmental periods and why the developmental perspective is always to be kept in mind. As described above, what might seem manic-depressive mood changes in an adult are often the norm in adolescence. An element of bi-polar symptomatology in adolescents can be alarming but needs to be handled with care, as it is so much less obviously a sign of pathology than it would be in an adult. This does not imply that such symptoms may not be serving the same psychodynamic purpose, but it might well influence how serious one assessed the problem to be (Waddell 2002).

Similarly, what would be worryingly conformist in an adolescent, such as an overriding worry about breaking rules, would be more normal in an 8 year old. What would be fine in a 9 year old – for example, an intense cataloguing interest in different makes of cars – might be worrying and an indicator of much more serious psychopathology in an adolescent.

There is a wide range of what can be expected and still deemed age-appropriate in terms of both behaviour and interests, and of course cultural differences must be taken into account, but one can only assess the depth of disturbance in a young person or be accurately attuned to the prevailing anxieties by using the reference points given by an understanding of normal emotional development.

# 6

# LEARNING – THE HARDEST TASK OF ALL

All children, by definition, are in the business of learning. Learning in the educational sense is an essential part of their experience but in addition the fundamental tasks inherent in being a child are to learn in a broader sense about themselves and their world and thereby to develop into an adult. Psychodynamic and psychoanalytic theory is centrally concerned with the emotional aspects of learning and the conscious and particularly the unconscious barriers that can impede it (Salzberger-Wittenburg 1983; Youell 2006). Much psychoanalytic literature centres on the difficulty of learning from emotional experience and being able to think (Bion 1962b; Britton 1987), which are obviously far wider issues than learning in the formal sense, but these theoretical contributions are relevant to both kinds. Learning is a complex process for all of us, fraught with the emotional conflicts around dependence, taking in from others, tolerating not knowing, coping with failure, managing success and digesting and making use of what we are 'fed'. For children who have experienced trauma, deprivation and inconsistency in their early life, the process is made extremely challenging.

We can think of these difficulties at different levels. For a child to learn they first and foremost have to have a mind – in the sense of having mental space and the mental capacity to have thoughts and make links between those thoughts. Developing a mind that can take in experience and make sense of it is a major achievement, and one that is made more or less problematic, depending on the quality of one's emotional experience right from the beginnings of life. It is endlessly fascinating to observe how an infant moves from being an entity that is experiencing a bombardment of physical sensations and bodily events into a little person with emotions, thoughts, memories, a personality and relationships. It is a complex and delicate process and one that can easily be derailed or distorted.

One needs to have a primary carer, let us for simplicity's sake suppose a mother although it may not be, who is herself capable of thinking and managing her emotions sufficiently for 'mindful'ness to develop. If the mother is able herself to hold on clearly to the fact that her baby is developing a mind, ascribing meaning and intent to his communications, being able imaginatively to enter into the baby's experience, then the stage is set for the baby to lay the foundations of his own mind and capacity to think. This is manifested from very early on, in the familiar way in which an attentive mother talks to the baby as if he understands, long before words are grasped, and when she attributes meaning to his noises and expressions long before the baby is making intentional communications.

How much a mother is able to keep guessing what the baby is feeling, and how much she manages to 'listen' to how he is himself experiencing his world, makes a very big difference. Even if a mother has to do something uncomfortable for the baby, like give him medicine, or undress him in a cold room, if she can empathize and let him know that she is aware of how he might be experiencing this, it will mitigate the discomfort a little and let him know that she knows he has a mind and a 'self' that is his very own. However, if the mother is feeling so persecuted by their infant, or has projected so much into the infant that they are not able properly to experience the baby as a separate person, it may be difficult for the baby to experience themselves as properly 'thought about' and this will interfere with their ability to think.

Every mother projects into her baby. She needs to idealize him in order to manage the enormous upheavals of early motherhood, and she needs to see him as being in possession of all that is best and most precious in herself in order to devote herself sufficiently to him and to be able to meet his needs despite her exhaustion. However, she can also project a great deal more than this, including more problematic elements of herself. This is especially going to be the case if she herself is not getting enough support from the father or other important adults. A mother's ability to offer what a baby needs is not just a matter of her own capacities but also crucially how well held, thought about, understood and looked after she also feels. She will also be drawing on all the powerful yet unremembered experiences of her own infancy, and will not find it easy to make available to her baby resources which she herself was never offered as a baby.

At times of feeling overwhelmed a mother might attribute to the baby manipulativeness and malevolence of which he is quite incapable. When feeling inadequate she can experience him as judge and jury finding her guilty or as a living embodiment of and reproach for her failures. Babies can unwittingly represent hated siblings, critical parents or other figures from her inner world. These and other projective fantasies can prevent her from being able to be aware of and attuned to her baby as a separate little person, as he has become a carrier of her own projected conflicts and fears.

Babies of mothers or other carers who have been massively projected into can have grave difficulties in developing sufficient space in their minds for them to make sense of their own experience and to become active agents in their own thinking. If mother is too bound up in her own painful state of mind she may find it difficult to let herself think about what baby is experiencing. If she is furthermore feeling guilty about how she is looking after the baby then she is likely to be too persecuted to allow herself to enter imaginatively into his world. A vicious circle can easily develop. The internally preoccupied or harassed mother cannot attend sufficiently to the baby's own experience; she then feels guilty and persecuted by the sense of not being a good-enough mother, and may unconsciously blame the baby for this horrible feeling. The baby will need to send out stronger signals to try to reach her and elicit what he needs from her, which could increase her sense of persecution. She may attribute to the baby deliberate cruelty, as if the baby is punishing her for her failings, when the baby is much more simply expressing some ordinary discomfort. The mother may therefore not tune in at all well to the baby, misperceiving his communications and either then ignoring or responding in a way that is not consistent with the baby's actual experience. As well as being powerfully emotionally distressing and destabilizing for the baby, this kind of experience, if repeated regularly, will disturb the development of the baby's sense of his own capacity to make and understand meanings. His own mind will not develop as well as it could, as he is given so much less help in working out what he is feeling and how to make sense of his inner life. Babies are both enormously vulnerable and astonishingly resilient. They often are capable of making the most of whatever mother and those others around them can offer, and can often recover well as and when there is more available to them. However, their capacity to establish a reasonably secure self within which thinking and learning can take place depends on there being a good-enough environment for this early emotional development – for them truly to have a mind of their own.

Once the baby has established this mind of his own, he then needs to learn how to use it. This again can be powerfully affected by the behaviour of care-givers early on. We can see how this can work in a very ordinary example from a baby of about 6 months. Arjun has picked up a small box that has a lid on it. He pulls at the lid, trying to get it off. It does not yield, but he tries and tries again. He passes it from hand to hand, looking at it hard. He puts it down and seems at a loss, almost crying. His mother sees what he is doing, and she talks to him about it being difficult, and how frustrating it is when things don't work the way we want them to, but encourages him to try again. She passes him the box, holding it at the angle that will make it easiest for him, and tells him it will come off. He has another go, and this time it works. He smiles in triumph, holds it up for her to see, and then puts it on and takes it off again another few times.

Here Arjun has learned several extremely simple, everyday but important lessons. He has learned that trying again can make something happen that did not at first. He has learned that he is in fact capable of something that he had given up on and that it is worth persevering. But even more than this, he has learned that the feelings he had have been understood, that his mother has an understanding of what he was going through, and that she is able to tolerate his frustration and lack of competence in order to help him move on without herself taking over or making him feel worse.

Another mother who was herself tired, persecuted and harassed, at the limit of her own capacity to manage frustration, might have reacted differently. At the most benign end of the spectrum she might have just taken the lid off for him to do away with the cause of the upset. Or she might have taken the box away and given him something else for him to play with as it was upsetting him and this seemed kinder. Both of these would have deprived him of an opportunity to learn. But it might have been more problematic than that. She might have just reacted to his upset and crossness, and become annoyed with her son for being unhappy, as all she wants now is a bit of peace and quiet. In this she would be responding to him not as a mind, not as someone trying to figure something out, but as an unwelcome impingement on her, who maybe reminds her too much of the things she feels unable to manage at the moment.

There will be times when every mother responds in this way, but if it is systematic then the baby gets little support for the learning he is trying to do. He gets the message that it is his effect on mother that matters, not what is going on inside him. His frustrations and small triumphs are not noticed, not given meaning, so the curiosity that could have helped him become a more active learner is inhibited.

In an even more troubling version of this story, Arjun's mother might have laughed at him for being so incapable, projecting her own sense of inadequacy into him. Worse she might have teased him, showing him how to do it but not letting him try. In infant observations one sometimes finds mothers (who have often had cruel upbringings of their own) relishing the power over their infants in a way that easily turns into cruel teasing. They see their babies trying to reach things or to make an object behave in a certain way, but instead of helping or even just observing, they will instead mock their failures or tantalize them by continually moving things out of reach just as the baby is about to succeed. Such behaviour will have deep roots in the difficulties the mothers themselves have faced, but the effect on the child will be damaging whatever the cause may be.

In these early experiences lie the foundations of having a mind and being able to use it to figure things out. Much can go wrong with this, even if the child is not actively traumatized by abuse. For those children who have actively been abused, the dismantling of their ability to think and of the possibility of meaning can be a defensive manoeuvre to cope with experiences that are not think-about-able (Sinason 1992).

A child's potential to learn therefore involves having a mind capable of thinking and capable of bearing frustration enough to keep trying when things are hard. However, there are still many obstacles to overcome in order to become an effective learner. The child also has to be curious, to actually want things to make sense. If a baby is brought up in a 'good-enough' environment (Winnicott 1953), within an atmosphere of care and with a relatively calm and robust carer, who is themselves thoughtful and interested in their baby, they are going to be able to be curious about the world. What Klein called the epistemophilic instinct (1923) is there from the beginning, starting with a curiosity about the mother and then spreading out to encompass a wish and a need to find out about the family and thence the outside world. However, if the baby is met with a mother whose inner world is full of persecutory feelings, or a depressed mother who emanates a sense of deadness or damage, or if the baby's natural curiosity is itself experienced by a mother as intrusive or disruptive, then the baby may learn not to be curious.

If what could be found out emotionally by looking more closely at the world, or looking more closely into their mother's mind, is felt to be dangerous, then the baby may get to feel that finding out is not such a good idea after all. Paul (11) was referred for help with educational delay. He had been brought up for his first two years by his mother who was mentally ill. He was taken into care and adopted when she suffered a psychotic breakdown and was hospitalized. He was not unintelligent but showed serious learning inhibitions and delays. He could learn things by heart and manage simple 'knowledge' but was not good at making links or exploring anything in any depth. In his counselling he made numerous boxes and houses that had no doors or whose windows were always shut. When he finally managed to make a house that could be entered there was a terrible monster inside. One reading of this material is to infer that there was a huge embargo on curiosity. Looking or going inside was too dangerous. It simply was not safe to try to find things out. This had inhibited his relationship with learning from very early on, and even though he was not overtly an anxious boy, a fundamental anxiety about the nature of the world had led him to keep his engagement with it at a superficial and limited level.

A child therefore needs a mind, capable of thought, capable of managing frustration and capable of curiosity, before he can effectively learn. Beyond this are further hurdles though. Being able to learn from a teacher involves the capacity to trust and take in from an adult, which in itself, regardless of the subject matter, is not easy for many children. It is maybe even more complex for an adolescent who is deeply ambivalent about dependence. It involves being able to accept one's junior status and accept the generational boundaries and differences. This is never easy and can arouse intense difficulties and tensions. If the adults in one's life have been, or have been felt to be, untrustworthy and unworthy of respect, then these difficulties will be readily transferred to any teacher, especially if they are experienced as inconsistent or felt to be unfair. Being able to accept being small and vulnerable can be unmanageable for some children and young people for whom this state has already been found to be intolerable. Omnipotent defences can step in, originally designed to protect the vulnerable child from intense anxiety, but now preventing the child from growing and progressing.

Learning involves not just taking in from someone else, but first and foremost tolerating the fact that one does not already know or understand something. It takes an inner confidence and solidity to be able to acknowledge sufficiently what we don't know so as to be able to learn about it. Not knowing is laden with feelings of vulnerability, and defences against it can mean that a child clings to certainties and cannot allow room for new understanding. Even as adults, we can find it very unsettling to realize that there are important things we have not understood, and to be open to new learning at any age means forgoing an idea of ourselves as competent and 'on top of things' (Taylor 2001). Even adult learners can find it very difficult to accept that our knowledge and understanding is limited or even wrong. Every time one picks up a book or a journal to further one's understanding of one's professional role, there is a conflict between the part of us that wants to learn and the part that would like to think we know what we are doing. Every new idea means a rearrangement of what we already know, and the acceptance that we have never reached the end of our learning (Taylor 2001). For those children who have not been helped to bear their feelings of confusion or ignorance, whether primarily because of early traumatic experiences or because of internal factors, the state of not knowing can be unmanageable.

As we as adults also know very well, learning is also bedevilled with the need to manage envy. It can be difficult to read what someone else has written or study someone's discoveries because we wish we had written it/discovered them ourselves, or because it is too painful that someone else has talents that we do not have and cannot emulate. I have to be in a fairly robust state of mind to pick up a professional journal and read what my colleagues have been working on. The desire to learn can be easily inhibited by the fear of being made to feel less able or the envy of those who are so much better equipped. Many of us learn less than we might because it hurts to acknowledge how relatively little we are capable of compared to those from whom we could learn. Every professional presentation or conference can bring conflict between admiration for the skills and understanding of others and the possibility of an envious attack on what they are giving us. Children are less likely to have these feelings available for conscious thought, but their envy of adults who seem to have things under control and of those who have the creativity to have so much to offer in their texts or in their other productions can be cripplingly intense.

One teacher at a school for children with emotional and behavioural difficulties was devastated when the carefully prepared materials she had left out during break for the following lesson were trashed by her class. She had chosen an exercise she knew they would enjoy, and could not understand why they had been so destructive. There were perhaps many dynamics at work here, but one was envy, especially acute as this happened just before the end of term. The teacher did have a lot to offer, and the children could sense this. However, rather than it making them appreciative it filled them with envy and a sense of exclusion. She had something they wanted and needed, and she could choose to give it or with-hold it. This in itself was intensely provocative to this group of very deprived and mistreated children. It was just too hard for them to let her feel good about what she was giving them, just as she was about to take all that away for the long holiday, so they chose to disparage and destroy it instead. Then at least they might not have to know so keenly what they were going to be missing.

Adolescents who are scornful and disparaging of the books they have to read or the discoveries of others they are supposed to study may often be in the sway of such unacknowledged envy. Even if outwardly confident these young people are unconsciously aware of how far they have to go in order to achieve creative adulthood, and just as they can defensively despise the adults in their families or schools, they can be in the grip of destructive contempt for the material they have to study. Whatever is difficult or challenging can so easily be passed over as boring and irrelevant. Of course a good deal of what is learned in school has its 'boring and irrelevant' aspects to it, but a child who is keen to learn can put up with this and find some aspects of the work interesting or worth engaging with. A young person who is overcome with envy and an inability to manage being less able than someone else will find it only too easy to make out that such learning is beneath them.

Learning is always a relationship issue, whether with the teachers and parents around the young person or with the material and its creators (Salzburger-Wittenberg 1983; Youell 2006). Learning is about developing and moving into adulthood and independence, and so another related element of difficulties with learning can be if the child or adolescent has become enmeshed with a parent and separation has not been well established.

As an illustration of one aspect of this, Tyrone (11) was in the grip of a particular difficulty that can at times occur for boys brought up by single mothers. He did not seem able to respect or take anything in from teachers. One could perhaps have put this down to the diffi-culties his mother had in managing boundaries and discipline in the home, without a partner to support and back her up, which was definitely a feature, although of course this can be the case in two-parent families. However, what seemed more important was that without a father at home there had been much less chance for Tyrone to work out where he fitted in, in relation to his mother, or in psychoanalytic terms one could say that the Oedipal situation had not been well worked through. In such a situation the child has had less chance of having truly accepted his place in the world, and so allowing teachers to have something to offer him was very challenging. Tyrone seemed to have difficulties in knowing what 'size' he was, seeing it as his job to protect his mother and be the man of the house, and was covering great vulnerability with a fantasy of being all that his mother needed and certainly in no need of anything himself. Children like Tyrone are particularly at risk of feeling that a gang-style relationship will offer them safety without needing to admit vulnerability, and of feeling that any dependency on an adult will be a catastrophe. A young person has to have the capacity to let someone else be important to them or they will not be able to make good use of school.

Another kind of difficulty is when the parents unconsciously (or even consciously) cannot manage their child growing up (see Chapter 10). The child may be an actual carer, or more often an unofficial carer in the sense of the family unconsciously relying on this child to meet the needs of the parents by not developing too far or too fast. This can be an issue for those who are the youngest, as their maturation can carry the unthinkable message that the children have grown up and the couple will be on their own again, or the single parent will be literally on their own. It can also be an issue for the eldest, if they are the first to confront the parents with the ideas around children growing up, with what this brings into awareness, such as the inevitability of separation and eventually mortality. Some families are engaged in elaborate unconscious avoidance tactics around these issues and the child may find that they are sabotaging themselves in the service of a family dynamic that is holding them back.

So far we have only been looking at general difficulties in learning. There are also going to be many times when a child or adolescent is having a problem in some specific area. There is an extensive literature by psychotherapists and educational therapists illustrating how for some children there can be unconscious meanings that prevent their being able to learn well in particular areas. There was 7-year-old Sally who could not manage subtraction sums that before she had been able to do well, which turned out to be about the fact that her father had just left the home. 'Take-aways' and 'difference' sums suddenly flummoxed her and she kept making mistakes.

Father having been 'taken away' and her whole life being different now he was gone was such an overwhelmingly difficult experience that this ordinary mathematical activity defeated her. Similarly Tyrrel (6) had major difficulties with additions following his mother's remarriage which brought two step-siblings into his life. More and more had been added against his will to his family, which to him had been in one sense an idyllic one-to-one with mother. His mind seized up at the thought of adding anything to anything.

Sometimes a particular subject can arouse very specific anxieties. The child may have no conscious knowledge of why they cannot write this particular essay or why they haven't remembered to do that assignment, but one can discover unexpected unconscious links that make sense and, once they are out in the open, bring about release for the child from their paralysis. For example, history was a surprisingly fraught subject for Lani whose own family history was full of dangerous knowledge, particularly powerful because not spoken about. Curiosity about the past for children like her may feel very risky and arouse what can feel to be odd resistances. Particular books studied in English can summon up internal ghosts and conflicts that lead to avoidance or stuckness. For example, Garth (14) found Hamlet near impossible to write about, having previously excelled in literature studies. In counselling it turned out that the theme of a father having disappeared in murky circumstances, and stepfathers being hated, was just too close to the bone. He had not been aware of this, but when his family circumstances were explored and the parallels noticed it suddenly made sense to him. Some children from mixed heritage families or from families with complex stories involving migration and separation can find geography unexpectedly difficult. Shoni (11) was one of these. Her family had had to flee their home country in appalling circumstances, leaving several members behind. Others from the extended family had gone to different countries, and there were painful mysteries still about where some had ended up. The map of the world for her was a minefield of undigested emotional trauma for her and her family, which perhaps made some sense of why geography homework nearly always got lost or was forgotten.

When a child comes to counselling with learning problems in the referral story, there are many ways to approach an understanding of what is going on. There may be global difficulties in thinking, in playing with thoughts and linking them together. Or there may be general problems about the relationships involved in learning: taking in from adults; managing not knowing; allowing others to be important; or to have 'got there first'. There may be overall concerns about succeeding and moving on. But on top of these and the other similar areas considered in this chapter, there may also be specific difficulties in relation to particular areas that have an as yet undetected and unconscious meaning that prevents the child from managing this particular piece of learning.

Everyone working with children needs to have some understanding of these issues as, whether or not one is explicitly connected with the child's educational life, the difficulties experienced in learning will be intimately bound up with the child's difficulties in their emotional life, and tackling one without an understanding of the other will lead to much wasted effort at best, and increased disaffection and waste of potential at worst.

Furthermore, most of the areas of difficulty considered in this chapter relating to learning in an educational sense are strongly implicated in the taking in of what a counsellor can offer. Understanding what can get in the way of learning gives one insight into the obstacles to the children making good use of us and the help we can provide. Learning is as much an emotional as an educational achievement, and allowing someone to make a difference to one's internal world – itself a complex kind of learning from emotional experience – can arouse the same sort of difficulties and defences.

# 7

# USING PLAY AND ART

Work with children, especially of primary age, is unlikely to take the form of simply talking. The counsellor needs to provide the child with equipment that can be used to express what is going on in their inner world, and to be able to understand the language that the child will use. This means being able to decipher how play is used to express what is going on unconsciously, and how art and craft may be understood as direct routes into the internal world, much as dreams can be used with older clients.

## Reading play

For children, play is a serious business. Especially for younger children, play is their work, the stuff of their lives. If one wants to assess an adult's functioning, one area of great importance to look at will be his capacity to function at work. Together with an assessment of his relationships with others and with himself, this will be a good guide as to what is going on inside him. For children, any assessment of how they are functioning should include a detailed look at how they play.

Furthermore, play is the activity where their inner worlds are brought into an interaction with the external 'real' world. Play occupies what Winnicott (1953) called 'potential space' between the child and the external world. It is neither wholly inner nor wholly outer, it takes place in between. As such, it offers a unique insight into the mind of the child. Watching a child at play can, if we learn how to see, show us many different layers of the child's psychological make-up.

Children use the opportunity to play in different ways. One very common use of play is for the children to enact and thereby gain some sense of mastery over what happens to them, as in the often seen schoolteacher or doctor role-plays. The children can thereby enter and control the adult world for a while, making either dolls or other children into the recipients of their own experiences. This can apply to good experiences, for example if doll babies are lavished with maternal care, but can be an effective way of digesting, of metabolizing anxiety provoked by experiences that have been difficult in one way or another, if the dolls are shouted at or given an injection. It is the child's way of ruminating as an adult might, but in action rather than thought or words.

Children's play is not in any simple way a direct copy of their life. The scenes portrayed may be close to what has actually happened, but equally they may not, as they may be an amalgamation of actual experience with the pressures and forces deriving from within the child. A bullying or punitive parent in play may indeed represent the child's experience but should never be read as a straightforward description, as it is filtered through the child's own emotional state and capacity to perceive the world, which may be distorted by the kind of inner world they inhabit.

Play is also a way of trying out identifications. The child can become anyone they wish in play, and can, in fantasy, learn a bit of what it feels like to be in a different relationship to the world. Long before they can shift their relationships with real people they may be able to explore different relationships in their play. They can be father, mother, superhero, teacher, witch, counsellor, policeman, or anyone else they choose. Often the child may play out being in a far more powerful role than he inhabits in real life. This may be seen as a defence against feelings of powerlessness and be used to project helplessness into the counsellor or the toy object of his tyranny. However, the aspirational as well as the defensive aspects of their play need attention (Alvarez 1989). We need to make room for the child's tentative hopefulness that there could be a time when he could have more mastery and a better sense of himself. Playing at being big is often a step towards growth, although it can also be a defensive response to being small.

In play, a child can allow all his destructiveness and rage free rein, secure in the knowledge that nobody is actually getting hurt. The whole world can be exploded and everybody killed, and yet all can come to life again. Daddies can be reduced and conquered, mummies blasted into oblivion, siblings dispatched, but without the threat of any of this being borne out in reality. Unconscious and secret wishes can be played out with toys, without the child ever quite losing touch with the knowledge that it is make-believe and therefore without encountering all the guilt or fear that would accompany any actual attempt to act out fantasies. Pretending to be, for example, mummy with a baby inside, may well indicate envy and admiration on the part of the little boy, but it does not in itself mean he does not want to be himself. It is also in most cases a step towards coming to terms with being a boy and having one's own role to play eventually in grown-up life.

In counselling the first and most critical aspect to look at will be the child's capacity to play at all. Some children will be too frightened or inhibited to play, others will want to attack or bully rather than embark on play about attacking and bullying. It can be a mark of great progress with a child if, instead of throwing things at the counsellor, they begin to be able to get action figures to do the fighting. The capacity to symbolize (Segal 1957) is a crucial first step to being able to reflect and be more mindful about what is going on inside.

The quality of the play, rather than simply the content, also needs to be carefully observed. Is the child able to let stories develop in his play, or are the toys controlled so tightly that they can be lined up or arranged but not given a plot to follow? Is there any clear story line or is it all hopelessly confused and random? Can the play be followed to a conclusion, or does the child break off in the middle because of some anxiety or because the feelings suddenly become too real? As an illustration, Elena (6) used to line up the toys and spend ages just adjusting their positions. She could add another to them or take one away, but nothing ever really happened. The point of the play seemed to be to prevent anything from occurring. Later in the work she began to allow the toys to move about individually and to travel around the table, so long as they didn't interact. Gradually the toys began to interrelate and relationships began to emerge. The fear behind the early rigidity became clearer as the toys began to fight and to develop complex and destructive attitudes towards one another, often resulting in the children dolls being eaten up by the wild animals. But now at least the fearful fantasies were being explored in the presence of the counsellor and the toys increasingly came to life for this little girl – dramatically enacting her anxieties but also enabling them to be thought about.

We need to attend also to the diversity of the play. If play is repeated over and over again, it can mean many things. It might mean that the play contains something vitally important that cannot be left until it has been understood and worked on. More thoughtful attention to the meaning will then enable the child to move on. However, repetitive play can also mean that something that could be available to the child in the counselling is being killed off. The point of the play is to limit and restrict the possibility of meaning or increased communication – and it will be this that needs understanding rather than simply the content of the play. There is a deadness to this kind of play that can usually be detected, but if we are striving too hard to pick up the meaning of the content we may miss the more informative emotional atmosphere around it.

By watching play one soon gets an impression of what kind of internal figures dominate the child's world. In some children's play the odds against them are overwhelming and the good figures are not strong enough to prevail. Or maybe they do win out in the end but only by recourse to magic and endless elaborations of superpowers. One will be able to see how much the play shows the child's capacity to address their inner conflicts, and whether the child has helpful or harmful inner figures at his side.

For example, Barry (10) made a stupid policeman get endlessly fooled and out-manoeuvred by various bad guys. It was a sign of progress and internal change when he acted a story in which the burglar fell in the water and the policeman helped him out. Shortly after this he enacted a fire in a Lego house, and a man rescued a boy from it. This echoed the fact that Barry himself had been rescued from a fire at 18 months. One could see that he had been enabled to get back in touch with his own vulnerability as a child who needed strong adults, instead of puffing himself up in illusory arrogant invulnerability which had, when acted out in his real life, led him to the borders of serious delinquency.

As mentioned in Chapter 3, the counsellor needs to learn how to observe play and when and how to comment on it. She also needs to work on whether and how to join in with play if the child wants to include her. There is a great skill in being able to be part of the child/s play without being taken over and controlled by it completely. Children will allocate the counsellor roles and we have to find a way of taking this on without either putting too much of ourselves into the role or being so stilted and inhibited that the emotional flow is prevented. We have to keep one foot in the game and one foot outside. This is true whether we are given a role to act out or allocated toys to play out a drama.

As an example, Talia (8) repeatedly told her counsellor that she was to play the part of the wicked witch. As the witch the counsellor had to cackle and scheme and to trap children (including of course Talia) in order to eat them. The counsellor felt uncomfortable playing this part, fearing that she would just confirm Talia's persecutory fantasies about her and other adults. However, she managed it by employing a few key techniques. Firstly, although she played the role with some gusto, so that the game had something of herself in it, she also stopped at different moments of the play to ask Talia in a whisper what the wicked witch was supposed to do or say next. This had the effect of keeping in both their minds that the true author of the play was Talia, without having to stop the game. The counsellor would play her part but not let the persecutory fantasy become too real by being too good at devising her own script for the cruel witch. Secondly, she commented from time to time on the action, and on her role, putting words and thought around both the dynamics of the story but also the way in which Talia was making her into someone cruel who hated children. When the witch was finally triumphed over by water being poured on her (as in the Wizard of Oz), it was possible to both play the part and comment on how the scary witch just melted away in the end and Talia could feel she had triumphed over her, thereby making the triumph clearly one over the witch rather than simplistically over the counsellor. Nonetheless it was important to note with Talia how good it felt for her to be the powerful one in the game, as in the counselling the holiday was coming and she might be feeling as if the counsellor was the one with the power over whether they met or not.

A counsellor can therefore creatively enter the imaginative world of the child, but without either taking over and steering the game in a direction more in tune with their own inner worlds, or being so sternly in the role of counsellor that they cannot play at all. The dynamics of the game can be used to explore aspects of the child's inner world, but the transference dynamics can also be kept in mind.

There may, however, be times when the counsellor might choose not to play actively with the child. This could be when the play is being used to close down thinking and prevent a closer encounter between child and counsellor. Or it could be when the counsellor is being given a role that they strongly feel would be beyond what would be helpful or involves acting out something actively abusive, such as tying a child up or perhaps throwing things at him. It is helpful then to put into words how uncomfortable it feels to be made into such a perverse character, and to resist the way in which the child is trying to force the counsellor into becoming something very different from who she is. It can be an immense relief if a child who has been abused in the past can be shown that some adults will draw a line that keeps their well-being in the forefront, despite that part of themselves that can be driven to recreate the abusive situation (Hunter 1986). The key issue will be around how real all this is for the child. Games can be played involving some pretty nasty behaviour, but both counsellor and child know it is not real, so can keep one foot in external reality during the game. But for some children the fantasy is very thinly separated from reality and then much more care needs to be taken.

Each counsellor will have their own style, and their own limits as to what they can manage in the way of play. They will also, as described above, need to respond to the particular state of mind of the child in deciding whether and to what extent they take part in games. They will need always to be keeping their psychodynamic thinking at the forefront of their minds, with an eye on the game, an eye on the child's inner world and a third (!) eye on the way in which the game is not only about itself but about the relationship between the child and themselves. If this is done well, then the playing in the sessions can be immensely valuable, both as a way of understanding the child and as a way of approaching the child's emotional reality together, with the added dimension of explicitly sharing the enterprise of exploration with each other.

## Working with art materials

Younger children will often use art and craft materials to express and explore their inner worlds, and a counsellor needs to develop a skill in 'reading' this in the same way as learning to 'read' play. Many of the same considerations apply in that it is as much the manner in which things are done as the content that is there to be understood. Careful, inhibited, hesitant drawing will obviously hold a different message about the child's emotional state from spontaneous free painting, which itself needs to be differentiated from manic excited splattering. However, there is much to be made of the content of the children's art work, and it is important to become adept at looking for the unconscious meaning of the children's productions. Alongside this it is essential to have a good awareness of developmental issues, for example the level of detail that can reasonably be expected at different ages (viz. the *Goodenough Draw a Man* test, 1926). If an eight year old draws a person without arms it means something more than if a five year old does the same, and may be telling us something about an inner object that cannot hold or reach him, for example.

It is impossible to do justice in this context to the richness and variety of children's capacity to express themselves in art, which has been the subject of study for both psychotherapists and art therapists for decades (Dalley 1984; Moore 1990; Case and Dalley 2008). There are nonetheless some general observations which may be of use. It is important to observe and try to make sense not just of the finished product but also of how a child builds up a picture, as the picture and its making is its own story and its own illustration of the flow of free association. However, it is also very useful to stand back at the end and look at the production as a whole. Often the picture will betray unconscious links in its entirety that is more than the sum of its parts. As a simple example, a child might draw a series of figures, not as part of one story but just as they come to mind. There might at the end be a telling range of sizes portrayed, with maybe the mother very small and a sibling huge, or the self tiny in relation to a large baby brother. In less obviously relationship-based work, there could be a way in which the whole picture, even if done in separate or faltering stages, demonstrates an important emotional message that was not evident as it grew up. For example, Isil (9) drew a house and put it to one side. Later in the session she was doodling idly, and created a large cloud of dark swirls in the corner of the page. By the end the house was being threatened by a massive dark shape, which belied her cheerful manner, and led to a useful opening up of her anxieties and misgivings.

There are particular kinds of imagery that appear repeatedly in children's drawings and paintings, which can be of great use to decipher. Pictures of figures and the portrayal of families are obviously important sources of emotional information and indeed can be asked for as part of assessment interviews in certain settings. As mentioned above, another recurrent image is that of the house. Almost invariably a picture of a house can be read as a self-portrait of some kind. The stereotyped latency child's house is of course nothing like the houses or flats they mostly live in, but it recurs as an almost universal image for very good reason. It usually has window eyes, a door mouth and a roof mind. Issues of access and availability are often signalled by the nature of the doors and windows, whether there are handles and letterboxes, paths to the door, gates and so on. Very large upstairs windows can indicate the need for great watchfulness or having seen too much, and tiny doors or large locks can indicate a difficulty in expressing oneself or a need to restrict access, as with children who have been either physically or emotionally intruded on (Williams 1997). Billowing chimneys can mean that there is a lot of anger 'up there' or puffs of smoke can be a sign that something is being signalled without words. One can go on at length, but the important message is that the nature of the house can often tell us a great deal about the child's sense of themselves in a number of dimensions.

Use of colour is another element in art work that can be thought about to great effect, and is often of great importance to children. Melanie Klein's patient Richard ended up having a whole cast of characters represented by different colours in his drawings (Klein 1961). It is vital not to jump to conclusions about the meaning of colours, especially if working with children from different ethnic backgrounds, as colours can carry different symbolism in different cultures. It is true that for many black might denote depression, or red anger and so on but care is needed as each child may have his own colour vocabulary. Nonetheless there is a general consensus on the emotional qualities of some colours (linked to the degrees of warmth in the colour wheel or obvious links to fire, the sun, etc.) that is often a good guide. There is also the degree of clarity of colours, the way in which they mix, meet, cover each other up or are made to stay apart, the rhythm of their interactions, the thickness of the medium, the range and freedom of their use, as well as the actual way they create an image, all of which can be food for thought as to the message unconsciously being conveyed.

Craft work is also full of potential for revealing the child's state of mind and inner configurations. Naturally the more sophisticated the skills needed to manipulate the materials the more this has to be kept in mind in understanding what is being communicated. A child who makes a large pot out of clay which then collapses is not necessarily telling us about the nature of his internal container, as it requires particular techniques to make a large pot strong enough to stay in shape. However, his attempt to make it and his reaction to the pot's collapse might be full of interesting information. A child who can paste junk boxes together to make a vehicle may not make it look much like a car, but if he can put disparate bits together into something that has a distinct shape of its own he is showing us something about his capacity to build a coherent self out of what he has been given. Most of us would find it hard to make a car out of these materials, so we have to take into account the level of difficulty of what is being attempted rather than just assessing the outcome. Nonetheless we need to take seriously what is going on with the child who endlessly attempts to make craft items that fail, who repeatedly uses materials that are not up to the task or whose creations are seriously incoherent. This kind of difficulty can tell us much about the inner despair or confusion with which the child is struggling. Or the continued trying can inform us movingly about the remaining hope that something can still be done.

Again it is not possible to do anything like full justice to the fascinating richness and symbolism of children's art and craft work in this chapter, but what is clear is that the counsellor needs to develop the ability to understand the unconscious messages using these media if they are to be able to tune in fully to the child and their inner world. The art work can become an essential part of a 'conversation' with the child, even if the child rarely speaks. One 12 year old I saw hardly ever properly talked to me, but would draw prolifically. I would interpret the drawing, and the next drawing was her 'reply'. The therapy was largely conducted using this kind of conversation and it seemed to work well. She improved rapidly as, without her saying much, we were still understanding together and working through the conflicts conveyed in her pictures.

Working with art both facilitates the children in working through their own emotional issues without having to put them into words – to do some all-important non-verbal 'thinking' – and also gives us a window into their inner worlds which can tell us so much more than it would be possible for them to talk about. It is both a way of communicating with us and a therapeutic medium in itself, with rich possibilities for freeing up the child's access to their own unconscious and for helping them encounter and work through their own emotional realities.

# 8

# BEHAVIOUR

When working psychodynamically with adults, there is a great deal to be observed in their non-verbal communications – how they enter the room, how they sit, what they wear and whether and how they fiddle with things. There may also on some occasions be more large-scale behaviour that requires attention – for example, if someone jumps up and paces the room, or hides their face, or perhaps even throws something in fury or walks out. However, these more extreme events will be relatively rare in adult work, where for the most part clients spend their sessions talking.

With children it is not like this. If children are playing in the room they are moving around, using the equipment, fully and physically interacting with the setting and with the counsellor. If they are playing ball or splashing water in the sink, they are using a physical language that most adults do not have ready access to. If children are angry, upset or otherwise in the grip of a strong emotion they will naturally be likely to express this through their behaviour, rather than tell us about it. Furthermore, many of the children who come into counselling are there wholly or in part because they have been unable to manage the behaviour boundaries established by teachers or carers in their ordinary lives, so we can expect that these issues will enter the counselling sooner or later.

The counsellor will be observing the child's behaviour all the time and using this in their understanding of the child, whether the child is in ordinary social terms behaving well or badly. A child's compliance and inhibition is just as noteworthy and worth responding to as a child's testing of the boundaries. It is easy to be lulled into an unquestioning place by behaviour that does not challenge us, when it is just as vital to question what kind of adult the child is relating to if they are being what they think of as good. Some children are desperate about their acceptability, and will be placatory and dutiful when underneath they are angry and frightened. There could be situations when the first time a child breaks the rules is a time for some celebration as it represents the ability to take a risk in the presence of an adult who is trusted not to retaliate and whose goodwill is relied on to survive the challenge.

This can be true even with teenagers. Bella (14) was late for the first time recently, having lost track of time in a lesson. I could have taken this up as resistance or ambivalence, which of course it often can be, but in the circumstances I saw it as a real sign that things were changing for her. Her depression, which had been suicidal at times and had led to her harming herself and writing herself off with violent self-denigration, had been beginning to lift. She had hitherto been totally absorbed in her obsessional self-hatred and the sessions had sometimes been caught up in this unhealthy and negative ruminating focus on what was wrong with her. Her being late was in this case a signal to us both that she was beginning to be reclaimed by the world of her schoolwork, which is where she most needed to be.

With Anisha (7), the first time she made a mess with the paints in the room was a cause of great relief for the counsellor. This little girl had been painfully careful, clearing up every trace of her presence from each little bit of play that she allowed herself. When she was able to leave the painting table with blobs of paint on the oilcloth and not wash her brushes, it was a sign that she was less afraid, more able to rely on someone else to manage the less acceptable side of herself and beginning to allow a livelier, less controlled aspect of her personality to show.

Over-good behaviour needs careful thought, but naturally the kind of behaviour that poses more of a problem for the counsellor is that which is directly challenging. This requires sensitive and thoughtful handling. When a child acts violently or dangerously, is destructive to the room or its contents, or runs out before the end of the session – these are actions that require a response from us and it can be very taxing working out what to do. When should we tolerate difficult behaviour and interpret it, and when is the appropriate reaction to set limits and stop it?

At one end of the spectrum we might feel that it is our job to allow the child to express himself to the utmost, and therefore that we should just permit the behaviour and do our best to find a meaning in what is being done. It is a frequent error made by inexperienced counsellors to feel that they should never set limits for a child. They feel that interpretation should be enough, and dread that if they set limits they will be becoming yet another repressive adult. Temperley (1979) is very helpful on these dynamics, although she is talking about social work interactions with adults. 'The most damaged … clients have inner worlds that are bound to be dominated by persecuting and attacked figures, and we hesitate to take positions where we sense we are likely to be seen in terms of these figures, to have these internal objects projected on to us.'

There will always be a reason behind difficult behaviour and it needs to be understood. Sometimes a child can hear our interpretation and will be emotionally able to respond by stopping. For example, Paulo (8) was filling his pockets and sleeves with toys just before the end of the session and saying he was 'taking the lot and you can't stop me'. His counsellor spoke to him about his needing to fill himself up as he couldn't quite believe that she and the room and the toys would still be here for him next time. He felt he had to steal things as he never felt quite sure that he would otherwise be given what he needed, but if he did steal them they never felt quite as good as if they were freely given. Paulo put the things back.

A good interpretation has put into words what has made the child greedy, angry, frightened, or needing to attack the room or the counsellor. The child has the experience of having had his feelings accepted understood and explained. The need for the behaviour passes as the driving force behind it is now 'think-about-able' rather than having to be acted out.

Adina (7) came into the room and went straight to the cupboard where other children's boxes were kept. She pulled hard at the handle, bashed at the door with a chair and then took scissors to the lock, risking doing damage to the cupboard and/or to herself. The counsellor suggested that she was showing her how shut out she had felt in the half-term holiday that had just passed, and was determined to attack the things of the children she felt had been able to see the counsellor while she couldn't. Adina didn't say anything but she stopped the attack and started to draw a picture of a nice house with a big gate barring the path to it. She was able to move from raw action to something much more symbolic, still on the theme of being kept out but not in a mode that was beyond the reach of real thinking.

There will be many other times when what needs to be understood is less the precise content of the behaviour and more the countertransference communication involved. We might, for example, be able to put into words that the child's wild behaviour is putting us in touch with what it is like not to know what on earth is going to happen next. This acceptance that the feeling is a communication of some aspect of how the child is experiencing their own world may be enough to help the child get some handle on their own feelings, feel understood and therefore manage to use less explosive means of expressions. Expulsive projective identification (Klein 1946) may give way to symbolic play, and a more manageable language can be re-established between child and counsellor.

There will be other times, however, when interpretation is not going to work like this. There will be boundaries that have to be set and adhered to. A child may be conveying how dangerous he feels and that no-one can manage his behaviour. He may be punishing us but not want to be able to destroy us. We must, when necessary, insist on the basic boundaries of the session. If we do not, we may be unconsciously communicating to the child that no-one is able to stand up to him, that his destructiveness is more than any adult can contain, and that also we are too weak or too afraid to help him gain more control over himself.

There is also a burden of guilt which we place on the children if we are unable to protect ourselves and the setting. Unconscious guilt is a most powerful force, and for many of the children their super-ego is far harsher and more punitive than we or the other adults around them could ever be. If we are unable to stop them from being destructive, we not only allow them to destroy what they need, but we also lay on them the guilt of having done so, which many of them will be unable to bear. Many disturbed children cannot bear the feeling of remorse, so utterly devastating is it felt to be, so their response to feeling that they have spoiled something is to go on an orgy of destructiveness – to drive themselves on to more destruction so as not to have a chance to pause and realize that they have done harm (Dyke 1985). If they look at us as counsellors and see people they have treated with contempt (or worse) with impunity, then they may not be able to face us and we may lose the chance to help them. As Temperley says, 'I suspect we may in fact lose clients precisely because at some level they are appalled by their aggression toward us and fear that we are incapable of recognizing it and helping them with it – that we are either too frightened to face it or that we will be so punitive that they had better avoid re-contacting us' (1979, p 7).

The need to set limits is not simply that room and person need to be respected, but that the dynamics of not doing so are unhelpful to the children (Phillips 1998). We need to convey to the children that we have self-respect, even if they or the adults around them do not. If we allow ourselves to be abused, how can they get the idea that they should not let themselves be abused, or that they should not abuse others to get rid of their terrible feelings? If we let them do things to us that are painful or humiliating, without responding in some robust way, then we are showing that we are too frightened to do so, or cannot tell the difference between being treated well and treated badly. We also need to show that we can tell when adults are needed to keep children safe, and that we will not allow them to put themselves at risk.

When Saida (7) is climbing on a chair balanced precariously on a table and jumping from one cupboard to another – what is her counsellor to do? Does she speak of Saida's need to be invulnerable and unafraid, does she talk about having to watch Saida put herself at risk, unable to keep her safe, does she wonder about the need to be high up – something Saida has used in the past as a metaphor for being grown up and 'above' the counsellor – or about Saida wanting to jump over the gaps – a reference to the holiday that is about to start? Or, does she tell Saida that what she is doing is not safe and that she cannot allow it to continue? Hopefully she will know Saida well enough to be able to judge whether interpretation will serve to bring the dangerous behaviour to an end, but she must be ready to set a limit if behaviour is risky. There can be room for both, with a firm limit set alongside some interpretation of the meaning of the behaviour. But if no limit is set and the interpretation is not received in a way that helps, then the counsellor is being put in the place of yet another adult who cannot help keep Saida safe or know when Saida is unable to manage this herself. Saida will not be helped by an adult of this kind, and an opportunity will have been lost to work on her omnipotence and the underlying terror of experiencing her vulnerability.

Similarly, the issue of running out of the room is a vexed one, and one that those who work with smaller children will be very likely to encounter. No-one wants to or should keep a child an unwilling prisoner in the counselling room, but neither can small children be allowed to run around unsupervized. The setting in which the counselling is taking place is a crucial component of the situation and what has to be taken into account in deciding on the best course of action. In schools there are rightly strict rules about this, and in a clinic it is often either unsafe or unacceptable to the others working there for children to be out of the room without an adult in close attendance. So what is the counsellor to do?

Yussef (8) ran out after he had thrown a car at his counsellor and hid behind a door in the corridor. The counsellor went to the counselling room doorway and said that she could see Yussef was worried that he had made her angry, but that she would like him to come back to finish the session and would wait for him to return to the room when he felt ready. Her calm voice and willingness to re-engage with him was enough to help him come back within a few minutes. Her refusal to be agitated at the situation or to threaten retaliation for the throwing was an eloquent statement that she had faith in her own and Yussef's ability to cope with his aggression. She was partly able to do this because she saw Yussef in a clinic where the waiting room and the receptionist's desk were between the room and the door to the outside. It was almost impossible therefore for Yussef to run out into danger.

However, it was a different situation with Paul, aged 6. He was known for running away and had been found on the street alone as a toddler. He found staying in the room very difficult, and at the slightest hint of uncomfortable feelings, would make for the door. His counsellor decided that she needed to position her chair partially in front of the door so that they could have a chance to think about the feelings rather than just act to avoid them. At first Paul resented this and tried to get past her, but before long he found that he could tolerate his feelings more and that her calm recognition of his rage and panic was sufficient to reduce it. She was showing that his anger and attacking was not beyond her capacity to bear or to contain. Moreover she was demonstrating something that he had not experienced sufficiently as a small child, which is the recognition that little children need adults to set safe boundaries for them, and that it is very frightening for a child to feel that his parents are unable to do this.

In between these extremes would be a plethora of different responses, depending on what is known and understood about the child, and what is manageable in different settings. Sometimes in extreme cases a colleague can be made available outside the counselling room to help a child return and to make sure they are safe if unable to do so. This is expensive in terms of resources, but can have the added benefit of demonstrating to the child that two adults can work together in his interests – again a situation which for very many of our clients has been lacking in their home lives.

Interpretation of what is making the child need to run out, or of what experience they are trying to offload onto the counsellor, whether primarily to evacuate it or to communicate it (Bion 1959), is often going to be important and necessary. However, in situations where this is not possible or not experienced by the child as helpful, the behaviour of the counsellor and the way in which they in their actions convey a message to the child about safety, robustness, hope, and a child's needs, will be an eloquent and hugely significant communication that goes far beyond words.

# PART II

# THE DYNAMICS OF THE COUNSELLING RELATIONSHIP IN CONTEXT

# 9

# UNDERSTANDING AND WORKING WITH GROUPS

Groups are powerful for all of us. They can foster the best in us and can bring out the worst. We are not the 'same person' in different groups, being steered by the culture of the group and our relationship with the task of the group into positions where different elements of our personality gain ascendancy. We all have a range of responses and defences that come into play in groups that may be considerably different or operate more strongly than in our more intimate and one-to-one relationships.

Children spend a great deal of their time in groups. School life dominates their week and their social life is often based around groups. Some children operate well in groups but seize up in one-to-one encounters, but more commonly children who can cope reasonably well in one-to-one situations become overwhelmed in groups, whether this is by the urge to act out in some way or by becoming inhibited and withdrawing. For many children, the presenting symptom behind referral is a difficulty with fitting in or functioning well in groups or with managing their friendships.

Some children like this might benefit greatly from work in a psychodynamic group (Reid 1987; Reid and Kolvin 1993). The problems they face will come into focus more quickly than in individual work. Individual counselling, even though it might help address the underlying difficulties behind the social problem, might also or even primarily, enable the child to take sanctuary and foster an idealized one-to-one that evades the key issue.

Counsellors may want to offer group work for a wide range of children with many different presenting difficulties. This may be for reasons of efficiency in that more children can be helped this way, but also because it can be an effective intervention for many children.

Group work can be less stigmatizing than individual counselling, it is more likely to be seen as fun (even though the children soon realize it is also hard work) and can be a good way of bringing into counselling children who might never take up the offer of individual work. It can be made much more ordinary, maybe arranged around publically recognized stages, such as a leavers' group at 11 or a transition group in the first year of secondary school. This means it can be perceived as relating to a shared moment in school life rather than to do with specific personal problems. On the other hand, it can also be offered to children who explicitly share a problem, such as anger management, essay or exam anxiety, bereavement or parental illness and carer responsibilities.

Working as a counsellor with a group can be very different technically from working one-to-one, but the underlying insight used in psychodynamic group work is much the same, with the addition of the psychodynamic understanding of group dynamics and group life (Bion 1961; Hinshelwood 1987).

The material we can use is extended as we not only have the individual child's presentation and the developing relationship with us to consider, but also how they manage their relationships with each other and the emerging preoccupations of the group as a whole. Over and above whatever explicit problems the children come with, the whole group will be wrestling with many shared concerns. They will all in different degrees be worried about their acceptability, about the ability of their carers to keep them in mind and to manage their difficulties. They will all be vulnerable to issues of connectedness and separateness, they will all have their own experiences and difficulties with vulnerability, trust and dependency. In a group, they will also directly bring issues of competitiveness and rivalry, as the group will elicit feelings of a sibling nature as they work out how to share the setting and counsellor. Any group will be filled with issues about individuality and membership, originating in the children's experiences of membership of their families, and so feelings with their roots in the children's family lives are brought vividly into being in the group experience.

A group gives the worker a wonderful opportunity to give the children both direct and indirect experience of these issues being addressed. They get direct experience of the counsellor's capacity to hold the setting and to keep searching for meaning in what every child does or says. They will have their own difficulties thought about and their relationships with others carefully attended to and understood. They get direct experience of an adult who keeps on trying to understand rather than simply reacting or retaliating or giving up. They can be helped to think about their responses to others and their difficulties in getting on with others. They can get a chance to work on the difficulties they have had with siblings and parents through the experiences in the group.

Over and above this, however, they also see the other children being thought about in the same way. They get not only insight but what has been called 'outsight' (Foulkes 1990) – seeing the meaning in someone else's behaviour even when maybe not quite ready to see the meaning of one's own, as a precursor to more personal insight. Our tolerance of and thoughtfulness about their own and others' behaviour in itself can create a space for their own capacity to think to develop. When they see us reacting with care rather than contempt for vulnerability in the other children, or when they see that an angry outburst by another child can be understood as a response to a vulnerable feeling, they can make tentative steps to integrate that part of themselves rather than having to project it.

They can get an experience of belonging, which might have been an area beset with difficulties in their families. In the group their absences are noted, their returns registered, their importance to the group as a whole acknowledged. Our ability to keep them all in mind and to treat their experience and behaviour as communicating something important will itself be of great value. Sibling relationships will, as mentioned, tend to be repeated and the other children will be cast in familiar roles from home, so that the same problems will arise in the group as are experienced there. This will mostly not be conscious, of course, but they will unconsciously be keenly attuned as to whether we fall in with their prescribed inner world dynamic. Insofar as we are capable of responding differently, both to their unconscious expressions of their inner world and to their 'siblings' in the group, we will be offering something powerful that can facilitate a loosening of the compulsion to repeat the same scenarios.

In a group, particular events or actions can be usefully understood, and real insight gained via our making sense of an event or a piece of behaviour. However, the therapeutic medium is going to be more keenly our maintenance of the counselling framework and a consistent attitude of mind. Maintaining our capacity to think and to contain, both in the prosaic sense of 'manage' and in the more psychodynamic sense of being able to bear and reflect on the transference and countertransference and group dynamics without being destroyed or provoked by them, is more likely to be the motor of psychic change.

For example, one group of four disruptive 9 and 10 year olds mounted a campaign of difficult behaviour in the group. It was difficult for the counsellor not to be goaded by their behaviour into becoming punitive. However, she was able to keep a firm insistence on the rules of the room (no destroying of equipment or hurting each other) while commenting whenever possible on their apparent need to turn her into a strict and punishing teacher whom they could comfortably hate, or alternatively see her as a weakling they could comfortably despise. She linked it to their own feelings of being small and unable always to cope, and how awful it was for them not to know what was going to happen next and to feel helpless when bad things were happening. She thought out loud about how afraid they were that they were too much for the people around them. This was especially relevant to two of them who had had spells in foster care.

These interpretations probably meant something to some of them some of the time. However, what made a difference was more her consistent willingness to keep thinking rather than fall into a repetition of their persecutory relationships, and her ability to show that she regarded what they did as a communication about their own feelings, rather than a judgement on her. After three weeks, during which the counsellor often indeed felt like giving up, the atmosphere changed. They were surprised she had not kicked them out nor cancelled the group, and although contempt and provocation still recurred, it never had that driven quality again. They stopped being a gang (see p 96) and became more differentiated as individuals as there was now room for other concerns to surface and be addressed.

## Projection and roles in groups

In a group, particular qualities and difficulties get projected into members with a valency for that characteristic, and we need to be alert to ways in which the group puts pressure on the members to act in particular ways, how the group 'elects' a member to speak for or to act out a concern or view that they all have some connection with. Each child will have his or her own character, but they will then be likely to have this used or misused by the group to relieve the others of responsibility for this element in themselves. So the child who is constantly testing the boundary of the setting may be acting for all the others, even though they profess to be annoyed with him. If one person is clearly the 'naughty one' or the 'shy one' then the others can split off that part of themselves and present themselves as being much less troubled by these issues.

For example, in a group of 8 and 9 year olds there was one child Peter who was often angry and aggressive towards the counsellor. He blamed her for everything, told her how useless she was and made fun of her clothes and mimicked her voice mockingly. The others sometimes joined in, but more usually distanced themselves from him, watching his behaviour from afar or occasionally getting upset with him for being so 'nasty'. They could be nice and cooperative with the counsellor in contrast to Peter, and appear much more respectful. However, the counsellor knew that many had difficulties of their own in dealing with adults in authority. She knew that Peter was speaking for them all in his need to defend himself against any feelings of neediness or dependence, and in his need for someone else to feel what it was like to be despised and thought to be useless. When he was absent after an exclusion it appeared that there was now a vacancy for Peter's position and, after a short while in which several candidates 'auditioned' for the role, a new member took up his position. Fortunately this could not only be observed but commented on, and the counsellor could therefore help them own their own feelings and difficulties to a greater extent, and also try thereby to prevent the new 'Peter' from being compelled by the group to get stuck in this position on their behalf. When Peter himself returned there was room for him to experience surprise and relief at being welcomed back and appreciation of the fact that he had been missed.

Another version of this kind of dynamic is when the group may be forcing one of their number to play a part in order to help them avoid something or to relieve them of a difficult feeling. For example, in a group of 11 year olds, Dwayne was always being disruptive by clowning around, interrupting serious discussions with jokes and silly faces. The others were ostensibly angry with him about this, and wanted him ejected from the group for preventing them from getting on with the work they wanted to do. However, one week he was absent, and the group as a whole became much more depressed and hopeless. They recognized that they missed his ability to poke fun at pain. They realized that, even though it had appeared that they resented Dwayne's misbehaviour, they had also been using it to keep at bay some difficult feelings. It is highly likely that Dwayne had been responding unconsciously to their need for someone to protect the group from these feelings and had not had much freedom to be different. His valency for silliness had been used by the group, and this aspect of him had become exaggerated. Once this was understood Dwayne was freed up to be in touch with and voice his own more vulnerable and sad feelings, without so much compulsion to become jokey and irreverent.

## Gang dynamics

Groups always have the potential to become gangs. Gangs are extremely effective at protecting their members from feelings of vulnerability and dependency on adults, offering an alternative 'family' to belong to that precludes adults from having importance or relevance. On the positive side they can give the child or adolescent a sense of belonging and of having support that may be, or may be felt to be, lacking in their family. In urban life they can offer protection when there is real danger and threat – indeed for some young people not belonging to any gang may take considerable courage. In working with groups, we need to be alert to gang dynamics as they may emerge, as they are powerful and potentially very destructive. In all group work one of the dimensions a counsellor can usefully be thinking about is the extent to which the group is acting as a group or a gang (Canham 2002). The children can become relieved temporarily of so many intolerable feelings if they gang up on an adult, so the temptation to do so is strong. Gangs divide the world into 'them' and 'us' in a way that all that is unbearable or unacceptable can be projected into 'them' and attacked there. In this way vulnerability and hurt can be given to 'them' by violence or bullying. 'They' can be rendered alien and subhuman and therefore out of reach of empathy. All feelings of powerlessness and lack of control over their lives can be projected by the gang into the 'other' by the gang's intimidation of those around them and by their imperviousness to adult sanctions. The pain of the infant that the child or adolescent has never been able to metabolize can be projected out into someone else much more easily, and internal persecutory feelings can be massively relieved by the persecuting of an external victim or the sense of being under attack by a rival gang.

In a group of children that one is working with psychodynamically, the fluctuations between gang and group functioning is likely to be an important focus. This may be between the children as a whole and the counsellor as in the example above, but it may also be manifested between the children. We need to keep a number of different issues in focus. Most importantly we need to make sense of what the children who are ganging up on us or one of the others are defending against, while also making it clear that we will not allow bullying. We also need to understand what makes the victim unable to make a better job of standing up to the gang, as victims are sometimes themselves projecting strongly, using someone else to carry their disavowed aggressive feelings. We need to reflect on how the behaviour is often specifically aimed at preventing thought, and preventing us from glimpsing and bringing more to the fore the anxious, vulnerable children who are hiding behind the gang dynamics.

Gangs demand a certain uniformity and can find differences unbearable. Differences bring unwelcome complexity into the frame and disturb the fantasized unity required to maintain the projection. A group, in contrast, can tolerate thinking, and can cooperate, even if not always harmoniously, in shared tasks. They can, even if with difficulty, manage there being differences between them, instead of turning differences into reasons for contempt or envy. They can even manage the fact that people leave the group, which is something gangs find particularly difficult. Once the children stop being a gang and become a group there is scope for much more differentiated relationships between them, and for them to discover parts of themselves that they had had to disavow in order to maintain their membership of the gang (Kegerreis 1993).

It has been said by Sue Reid (1999) that 'becoming a group is the therapy' and this means not only becoming more than a cluster of individuals, but also by implication avoiding being/ceasing to be a gang. This need for the children to be able to become functioning members of a group speaks to the importance for all of us of becoming maturely interdependent in a way that empowers our creative capacities and enriches both ourselves and society. This is central to managing ourselves in our adult professional and social lives. For the children we work with it is the key to being able to make better use of the milieu within which they are growing up.

Psychodynamic groups are usually conducted without an express task, either by providing art and other materials for the children to work with or with older children establishing a safe space for discussion. However, there can be tasks involved in the setting up of the group, such as the formulating of the group's rules (Cooper 1995) and the keeping of the calendar, around which the group can do collective work and explore its own nature. Beyond this, psychodynamic understanding can also be used with groups who are trying to fulfill a defined task, which may be appropriate if the group is convened around a particular issue or stage. Focused discussions,

joint story writing, picture making, music making, drama production or other activity can also provide an arena within which
psychodynamic thinking can become highly therapeutic, although
here the task itself becomes another overt 'party' in the dynamic.
There can then be room for the counsellor to think with the group
about what helps or hinders them in fulfilling the task, and how
their feelings about the task reveal their conflicts and anxieties over
their own creativity and capacity to cooperate.

In all groups, there is anxiety around whether or not the group
itself can survive and function, which has a dynamic of its own.
This speaks deeply to the children about their family experiences,
their sense of their own capacity to belong, and their feelings about
creativity and destructiveness, and these will be features that a
counsellor can be alert to whatever the express task the group is
convened to fulfill.

A group of primary school leavers was set up to create a large
painting as part of a celebration to open a new building in a school.
The children chosen for the group were all having difficulties of
different kinds in getting along with the others in their classes. It
was no surprise when these difficulties manifested themselves in the
joint work on the painting. It was intensely difficult for these children to cooperate. Nadil became more and more domineering,
intolerant of all the others having ideas of their own. Patti was her
usual quiet, submissive self, fading away into nothingness and often
not turning up for the group. Shanaz worked well for a while and
then destroyed her own and others' work. Carl moaned and worried
the whole time, despairingly pointing out how impossible it all was.
The counsellor used all this as a way of thinking about their anxieties about growing up, being able to contribute and hold their own
in secondary school. While she spent a lot of the time working
much as a teacher would, helping them address themselves to the
task, she also commented, whenever she felt it would be useful, on
the underlying concerns that the children were expressing through
their difficulties both with the task and with one another. It became
possible for them to think together about their worries about
whether they were good for the group task or bad, and about
whether they could be successful as an individual who was also a
part of something bigger. She could look at how hard it was to keep
believing that they collectively could create something of value. The
final product surprised the children in many ways, as it was a lively
and expressive piece of art, with significant contributions from each
of them, and their pride in it at the end was moving.

Thus group work can be an extremely valuable intervention as a therapeutic provision. Furthermore, psychodynamic thinking, including that applied to group dynamics, can be effective both in groups that are explicitly therapeutic and as an additional tool when working in groups that are engaged in less explicitly emotional work. If we can help children manage themselves in a group, and give them a chance to learn 'first hand about their impact on others' (Reid 1999), we can do so much to give them better prospects in their lives, both as members of a group and of wider society.

# 10
# CONSENT AND CLIENTHOOD

If an adult comes to a counsellor it is generally clear that the adult themselves is the client. Sometimes there is an element of legal compulsion or pressure from employers but generally speaking counselling is a voluntary activity by the adult who makes himself a client by seeking help. There are (important) arguments about how much the client is informed in his consent, in that he may not understand what counselling entails or what the 'contract' is going to involve, but at least he is coming under his own auspices and it is understood that he can withdraw at any time.

With children and adolescents consent is a much more vexed issue. Adolescents may indeed seek out help for themselves, and in community adolescent services the situation may be close to that pertaining to adults. However, in settings such as schools and universities, attending might not feel fully voluntary even if the adolescent agrees to it. They may be under threat of exclusion, or feel that they must attend counselling or face punishment. Younger children have almost always been referred for counselling by an adult, most usually a teacher, social worker or a carer, which may make it feel imposed and not voluntary for the child. Some may have been able to voice the wish to talk to someone, or to 'have someone to help', but they will not have much of an understanding of what counselling could involve so cannot fully be taken to have consented to the work in an informed way.

There are related issues here. First is the idea of consent, and how informed it is. This includes questions about parental consent – when it is needed and different ways of proceeding to get it. Secondly, there is the nature of the contract into which the client has entered and how this is explored or explained. Thirdly, there is the issue of 'who is the client' (Music and Hall 2008). Elements of this debate are factual or legal, but other elements are to do with how one can engage a child or adolescent in an active partnership in the work, even if they have been sent to counselling by someone else.

If a child is sent to counselling by a teacher, for example, the child will experience this as part of the school's provision, and this could have a variety of meanings. If the presenting problem is largely behavioural, the counselling can be experienced by the child as a punishment: a sanction relating to the bad behaviour. Likewise if a parent is sending the child to the counsellor because of a difficulty in relationships at home, the child is quite likely to see the counselling as either a punishment or, and this can be even worse for the child, a demonstration that the parent is defeated by the difficulties. Whatever the setting, even if the decision to access help is motivated by caring concern about a child's anxiety or distress, it will not always be welcomed by the child, as they may fear humiliation, exposure or an unwelcome intrusion. The counsellor has to take this into account when first meeting a child, and to help the child see the work as something they themselves want to engage with.

## Who is the client?

Schools and similar agencies which employ counsellors do so with the school's overall aims in mind, and therefore a school counsellor is in a real sense working for the school and not simply for their clients. The school is the overall client. This has many implications for the counsellor, who has to have in mind the educational progress of the child as well as their emotional development. Of course, helping a child with their emotional difficulties is almost always going to lead to an improvement in their educational functioning, so direct clashes are not going to be a regular feature. Nonetheless, the presence of the school as the overall client has its effect on the work and on the counsellor's frame of reference. This can be of particular poignancy in further and higher education, where attendance is voluntary, as the work in counselling could in some cases lead to a realization that the student is pursuing a course for reasons that are not in fact healthy for him, and that in getting to know himself better he realizes that he should change courses or leave. This may not be welcomed by the college or university.

In a school the equivalent could be a student realizing that he or she is pushing himself too hard in aiming for unrealistic goals, and this could lead to, say, the dropping of a subject or the lessening of an obsessional striving for excellence. Another possibility could be that the work could conceivably lead to a student becoming able to stand up for himself in relation to school or college authority in a way that the institution might not see as helpful. The counsellor obviously has to work hard not to take sides or become the client's champion (see page 136) but there will be some times when the work leads to an outcome other than that of a student more clearly back on the original chosen track. The school or college is the overall client but the needs of the child or adolescent in the work take precedence.

It is therefore important for the counsellor to have discussions with the school or college hierarchy to explore and explain how the counselling may or may not fit in with the school's expectations. It is better to have these issues discussed in general terms than to wait until a particular child's problems bring to light a discrepancy in expectations and assumptions that has not been aired earlier.

## Turning referrals into clients

There is more about the dynamics of the setting in Chapters 15 and 16, which go into more detail about some of these issues. What is relevant to this chapter, though, is that in whatever setting one works and with any client, there is work to be done to make a referral into an engaged client. In general terms, the older the child is, the more work this may entail. A young primary school child is more likely to welcome the fact that an adult is paying them special attention and giving them the space to explore their inner world through play. They won't always enjoy the sessions, as painful and difficult feelings will be explored, but they are more likely overall to experience the attention as benign, unless their interactions with adults have been extremely fraught in the past. Even so, important work needs to be done in engaging their interest in the work, and making them aware of what the work is for and about.

As already mentioned, they may well experience the counselling as a punishment for bad behaviour, and if so they will not be able to engage constructively in the work. Or they may feel that our interest in them is intrusive and unwelcome, threatening a precarious equilibrium that depends on denial or externalization for survival. Another possibility is that the counselling may feel like an invitation to a betrayal of family secrets and loyalties. This needs to be handled with great sensitivity and we need to stay as fully as possible engaged with the inner world of the child rather than seeking information too zealously about the external world. The real family of the child may be causing great concern, and there may be other agencies or interventions that need to address the outside world, but the family that counts most in the room is the internal one, and that one is always available, even if we know little about the real one. In one sense this is one of the greatest strengths of the psychodynamic approach. With its emphasis on the inner world, the transference and the countertransference, it enables us to address the conflicts and difficulties of the child even where we know little of the realities of the child's life.

Returning to issues of consent and engagement, whatever the age of the child, we have to develop skills in finding a way of interesting the child and tuning into their own perception of the situation, of locating their own worries and concerns, rather than being an extension of the adult who is sending them. We have to find a way of helping the child feel they are themselves the client, that there is work **they** want to do, rather than trying to 'fix' them for the teacher or carer.

For example, Tyler (8) was referred to the school counsellor because of his violent temper. He manifestly felt unfairly 'picked on' by the referral, and showed his resentment and sense of persecution at this openly in the first session. The counsellor talked with him about his temper, and gradually felt her way with him into how frighteningly out of control he himself felt when in the grip of his temper. She was also able to tune into how worried he was that he was too much for his parents and that he was going to be rejected by his friends. Once he had been enabled to experience the presenting issue as his own problem, rather than that of the grown-ups around him, he was able to engage much more wholeheartedly in the work, with a sense that he himself wanted to sort out the difficulties and understand what all the explosive anger was about.

Adolescents are often experts at exporting and projecting anxiety into others. They are past masters at making everyone around them worried while themselves being apparently blithely confident and content on the surface, if only the adults would get off their backs. This can make for difficulties in engaging them in counselling. It is a skilled job to reach behind these defences and to find a way of interesting them in their own emotional state and future. Marcus (14) started his first session with a sorry indignant tale of how he was seen as a bully. In his eyes he was being picked on and provoked, and had not said or done any of the things he was being accused of. He felt punished in having to come to counselling. The counsellor's early explorations led to the emergence of his deep sense of pain and deprivation relating to the death of his father. This had left him extremely vulnerable to casual slights, so he was easy to provoke. He was full of an un-think-about-able anger and indignation with the world for dealing him such a rough hand. By the end of the first session he and the counsellor had travelled a long way from the initial emotional reaction to the referral and had a viable contract to work.

The issue of parental consent is a vital but problematic one. With primary-aged children, parental consent should always be sought, and counselling should not be offered without it. In some cases this will mean that the child cannot be offered help even if the child themselves wants it. This is a painful difficulty to encounter, but to proceed without consent is not only clearly wrong but also unhelpful, as it would be bound to exacerbate loyalty conflicts for the child. Moreover, there needs to be positive support of some kind from home for the counselling to be something the child can use and integrate, and support is needed so that the child can encounter the pain currently being avoided through his symptoms. Gaining consent and support for the work might hopefully be something that could be worked on with the parents, or the refusal of it could be a signal that other interventions are needed instead of, or maybe in preparation for, counselling.

In schools, consent can be sought in much the same way as the school would notify parents of any other supportive provision of the school. However, if possible, the seeking of consent can be the opportunity to engage the parents in some new thinking about their child, and it can be a way of bringing the parents into a more thoughtful place in relation to their child's difficulties and emotional life. This is easier to achieve if the parents can feel as if their own worries and concerns are being heard and attended to, and the provision of some support for parents will greatly assist in bringing the parents into a better position for consent to be given for their child to be seen. The counsellor's capacity to engage parents either directly or indirectly will be much affected by the overall relationship between the school and the parents. If the school is generally experienced as benign and attentive to parents' concerns, then the offer of counselling is likely to be experienced as an extension of this. However, if the relationship between school and the parents is fraught, and full of mutual persecutory anxieties, then the offer of counselling is much more likely to be experienced by the parents as a blaming action by the school, or an avoidance of the school's failure to deal with the child's problems in a more ordinary way.

For example, Ali's (6) parents did not want him to be given counselling. He was being referred because he was so painfully shy and reserved, seeming anxious and finding it almost impossible to speak in class. Little was known about his family but the school thought that counselling might help him become a bit more secure and able to express himself. When a letter was sent home the father wrote a note saying they did not want anyone to work with Ali and blaming the school for not doing its job. The Special Needs Coordinator offered another appointment to see both parents to think about Ali's difficulties. These were cancelled twice but on the third attempt the parents arrived, together with a female cousin. It turned out that Ali's mother could not speak English, and the cousin was there to support and translate. Ali's mother was as a result cut off from mainstream British culture, and spent almost all her time at home. What emerged in the meeting is that both she and her husband had experienced the letter about counselling as a statement that Ali was mad or bad. They were private people, and the thought of someone they did not know seeing Ali intimately was highly unwelcome, as in their culture all family business was kept within the family. What also emerged was that Ali had been hugely important to his mother in the preschool years, all the more so because of her situation, but this meant that his starting school was a real problem for her, leaving her much more alone and isolated and without much of a focus.

Out of this meeting came a recommendation that Ali's mother attended English as a Second Language class for parents that the school was hosting. This helped with the English problem and also with the isolation that she was experiencing. The parents had a taste of the school being concerned about Ali in a way that was not to do with madness or badness and became less persecuted in their response. They consented to Ali seeing a learning support assistant to help him express himself, which helped, and later agreed to him having counselling.

In secondary schools, the issue of consent from parents is different, and less clear-cut, in that adolescents often want to access help without telling their parents. If the school has made it clear in their prospectus that counselling is part of the pastoral provision of the school, then it is neither a requirement that they be informed about the referral, nor that their permission is gained in advance. The Gillick competence findings (1985) apply here, in which under-16 year olds can consent to their own treatment if competent to do so.

There is the added proviso that counselling is not strictly speaking medical treatment but more a pastoral intervention from the school.

Nonetheless, the parents need to be in mind all the time. If a child is coming to counselling without parental knowledge, let alone consent, then this is a distinct feature of the work that needs to be attended to. It may be that the work needs to centre on the difficulty in communication in the family, with one possible aim of the work for the child to be able to talk about their difficulties with a parent. The possible splitting between the parents and the counsellor needs to be addressed, and work will have to be done to avoid some collusive alliance with the child. Furthermore, if the parents do not know about the counselling, there may be trouble being stored up for the future. Parents can be understandably dismayed and angry if they suddenly discover that their child has been talking to someone about their intimate business, and this can mean that the counselling can suddenly be terminated in a very unhelpful way.

On the other hand, counselling can sometimes be the only place where the child or adolescent can bring deep and frightening concerns that are about their family, when the family is unable to address issues. This may be when there is threatened or actual abuse, or when the child knows that the family cannot and will not allow discussion of their affairs with anyone outside.

For example, Cal (15) had a schizophrenic brother whose erratic behaviour periodically terrorized the family. The parents were deeply ashamed and protective about the brother's difficulties, and forbade any discussion of them with outsiders, apart from the doctor involved with the brother. It was a vital lifeline for Cal to be able to talk to a counsellor about the impact on him and his parents of this situation. He was terrified of being mad himself, deeply ill at ease with his own anger. It felt so dangerous, as in his mind it was linked with his brother's uncontrollable rages. He struggled painfully with his anger with his brother, his frustration and disappointment with his parents in their inability to manage things better, as well as his deep concern for their vulnerability. He felt guilty about being healthy, and also terribly burdened by his parents' need for him to succeed and to 'redeem' the family. His parents were (according to Cal) never going to give permission for counselling, but it was helpful to him that he had a space to process all this so as not to jeopardize his own future.

In another familiar situation, Kimmy (14) came to counselling to explore her anger difficulties and to work on her isolation from her peers. She was living with her father, who was barely coping as a parent, and she often had to care for him when he was drunk or depressed. He felt persecuted by any kind of communication from school, and Kimmy knew that he would not want her in counselling as he was against anyone knowing about the home situation. For Kimmy it was a huge relief not to have to manage so much on her own. The counselling gave her a space to process her feelings and to help her pay more attention to her own needs and teenage development, and to understand her own angry feelings without having to act them out so destructively.

There are other times when the child is adamant that the parents will not consent and should not know about the counselling but then, after some work on the inner conflicts and splitting going on in the child, it becomes possible for the child to start a different kind of conversation with the parents and tell them themselves. This a welcome and healthy development, as one way of conceptualizing the counsellor's job is to make it more possible for the child to use the others around them better, whether this be parents, teachers or friends.

For example, Shari (14) came to counselling in a very depressed state. She could not contemplate telling her mother how she was feeling, as she perceived her mother to be far too burdened and vulnerable herself. Shari felt guilty about how bad she felt, and thought that her mother would blame herself and take it as another blow if she knew. The counselling made more accessible to Shari how angry she was underneath the depression, and how much she nursed in her mind a grim but gratifying sense of having an unexploded bomb that she could set off at home at any time. The image of the mother being so vulnerable was not a complete fiction, but it was also a way of making sure that change could not happen. Imagined confrontations were constantly rehearsed but never brought into reality. Keeping how she was feeling from her mother was a way of maintaining a *status quo* that was deeply uncomfortable, but had within it the comforting idea that change was not possible and Shari's mother was always to be kept at arms length. It emerged that Shari was hugging to herself the idea that her mother couldn't understand her, as the feeling of hopeless grievance at least meant that nothing needed to be done, and her mother's failure was ensured.

Once these dynamics were explored, Shari was able one evening to tell her mother how she was feeling. She found to her surprise that her mother was already far more aware of what was going on than Shari had thought, and moreover was able to listen helpfully and they became closer as a result. There was then no problem in telling her mother about the counselling, and in fact Shari felt able to share with her mother some of what we had done together in a way that was not felt by her mother as an attack.

Thus informing her mother about the counselling and gaining her consent to it was in itself part of a healing process. Bringing the counselling into the communication with the parents and the acquisition of true consent is often a sign that much of the work is done. Consent is therefore far more than just permission – it is an ongoing dynamic between counsellor, child and parent that can have considerable power.

# 11

# WORKING WITH DIFFERENCE

Working with children in any setting is going to bring with it the need to consider carefully the child's cultural background and other possible areas of difference. This may give valuable insight not only into the child's world but also into how the child may be experiencing the counsellor, the setting and the offer of help. There will in many cases be important differences between the culture of the home, whether in terms of ethnicity, class or other dimensions, that are of great relevance to how the child sees the adults with whom he is dealing. This is different from the transference, in that it is not in a simple sense the projection of elements of the child's personal inner world of fantasy, but relates more to the real differences that the child perceives. The meaning of these will have conscious as well as unconscious dimensions.

After some serious neglect, the psychoanalytic world has been struggling harder in recent years to make sense of and address the difficulties of working with difference in the consulting room (Dalal 1988; Davids 1988, 1992, 1998; Williams 1991; Andreou 1999; Walker 2005; Foster et al. 2006). This nonetheless remains a highly charged and controversial area, to which we all need to attend with great care and continuous self-scrutiny. This chapter will take a brief look at how differences of race, culture, religion, gender, sexuality, class and physical/intellectual ability might need to be addressed in the counselling and some ways in which the counsellor can try to limit the way in which such differences can sabotage the work.

There are two distinct although overlapping areas that I am going to consider in this chapter: the way in which the perceived differences make an impact on the client's experience of the counsellor and the prejudices and blindnesses in the counsellor regarding the client.

When we are working as a counsellor with adults there is always one clear difference – that they are the client and we are not – and this is always there in the mind of both. It forms the foundation of the way we work and the meaning of it will be brought out repeatedly in our thinking about the relationship in the room. However, contingent on the particular identity of client and counsellor, it is possible that there would be otherwise not much difference between the two of us. In work with younger clients there will always be one other highly significant difference in the room, whoever the child is and whatever his background. This is the obvious one – we are adult and they are not. Despite being so commonplace, this also requires serious attention. It may sound obvious and unnecessary to single it out, but this is perhaps a mistake, as it can mean that it gets overlooked. It is easy for a counsellor, even if they are naturally aware of it, to leave this unexamined. We may then not fully take on board how the child feels to be relating to us, not in the specific way they perceive us personally, but as an adult *per se*.

If we can address this explicitly in the work we are already likely to make a better connection. Again this sounds so obvious, but actually it can be more of a challenge than we think and may be harder than we might like to admit. This may be especially the case if we are early in our careers and might not be in touch with how old we seem to our young clients! If our own adolescence seems quite recent it can be hard to admit that to the young people in front of us we are already seriously ancient and out of touch. This can get in the way of our acknowledgement and understanding that the life they are leading may be, in their minds, far away from anything we have experienced, and can lead them to be sceptical as to how much we are able to understand.

The issue of how well they imagine we can understand them is central to this area of concern. The more different we are, the more of an issue this will naturally be. If I am a 50-something white British woman with an upper middle-class accent, and my client is a black 15 year old who lives in extreme poverty and insecurity on a huge and intimidating estate, negotiating the gangs that dominate the area and threaten him daily, he is not going to think that I understand his life. The blunt fact of the matter is that he is right. I do not and indeed cannot understand what his life is like, if by this we mean that I can draw in any simple way on my own experience to relate to what he is telling me. I can still, however, do something to help him to think about his life, to work on how he manages the pressures he is under, to stay in touch with his own neediness and vulnerability, despite the blatant invitations to project and dispose of any dependent feelings. I can help him understand the conflicts that he himself experiences, and to negotiate a path that is congruent with his own needs as far as I can understand them. I can keep in mind the conscious and unconscious legacy from his family's past (Fletchman Smith 2000), but I will never know just what it feels like to live as he does.

It is worth thinking hard about who we are and how we appear to our young clients. We dress in a particular style, speak with a distinctive accent, use words of a particular complexity and length and carry ourselves with our own brand of confidence or diffidence. Each one of these features about us carries a cultural as well as a specific and more personal meaning. They brand us with a range of labels, all of which will have a different set of meanings for each child. The psychodynamic approach places strong emphasis on the transference, that is how the inner world of the child comes alive in the room and becomes a feature in their relationship with us and their perceptions of us. Unfortunately this can mean that at times we can miss the ways in which who we are and how we present ourselves has a powerful impact, which can skew and limit the perceptions of us that are available. This is particularly relevant in the early stages of the relationship when there has not been time for a more specific and personal transference to be built up and elaborated.

The simplest thing for us to do in the circumstances is to be prepared to be open with the child about how much he might doubt our capacity to understand his experiences, and indeed how much he might rightly doubt our having had any experiences of the same kind. It is much more helpful to do this than to try to pretend that we can be directly in touch with what he is bringing. If we have confidence in the value of psychodynamic thinking about any child's difficulties and the complexity of his relationships with himself and others, then we can convey that having had the same experiences is not a prerequisite for being effective in our role.

If, whether consciously or unconsciously, we feel that such common ground is necessary if we are to be truly helpful, it can be difficult to deal comfortably with the lack of it. It is difficult to get the balance right – realizing on the one hand that our clients are grappling with issues that we have (maybe mercifully) not had to manage and to respect their resilience and fortitude in so doing – and on the other hand having regard to how we can still be of use from our psychodynamic understanding.

I remember that when I was childless I felt indignant and hurt when the parents I was working with said or implied that I could not understand what they were experiencing in bringing up their children and therefore could be of limited helpfulness. I saw this as largely being a defence against using my thinking and psychodynamic insight. As soon as I had children of my own I saw it differently. I realized that I had indeed never fully understood what parents had been feeling about their children or about themselves as parents. This meant that I could personally sense the difference that having a particular set of experiences oneself gives to the work, and that such objections could not be dismissed as purely defensive, even if they could also be used defensively.

We need always to be humble about the extent of our capacity to understand the lives of those who have had radically different experiences, if by understanding we imply having any direct access to what they have gone through, Nonetheless, it is useful to remember that, even if we do share common features in our histories, it is always the particular meaning of experiences to our clients that matters, and this is never going to be the same for any two individuals. I could see that being a parent myself did give me access to some of the unique and intense power of the emotions involved in parenting, but it certainly could not tell me anything much about the way in which this has been felt by these parents with whom I was working.

There are, in fact, dangers in sharing too much common ground with clients, as well as difficulties in working across large cultural or other divides. Working with someone with a very similar story to our own, or whom we see as similar to how we were ourselves at that age, can lead to other sorts of blindness and problems of over-identification. If this happens we can be hindered in seeing the child in front of us clearly because we are seeing them through the lens of our own history and assumptions. Often unconsciously we can attribute to them issues and responses of our own, or be blind to difficulties as we too readily imagine that this person is like us. In a situation like this, supervision is going to more than ever be a key resource in helping us disentangle our identifications from genuine perceptions of the client.

## Culturally sensitive practice

Whatever the cultural background of our client we need to go in to each counselling relationship wanting to learn the particulars of the emotional dynamics for **this** particular child or adolescent. Only they can truly let us know what these are. Yet we also want to be alert to the meaning for them of their cultural background and their experience of being different from the counsellor. Thus there is a specific tension involved. On the one hand we might usefully want to understand more about, say, family culture in the Philippines, but we should never assume glibly that there is only one family culture there, nor assume by doing so we know anything very useful about this Filipino family. The danger of a little bit of knowledge about the culture we are dealing with is that it might lead us to make assumptions that are not helpful. The danger of knowing very little or nothing is that we might not know how to interpret the overall picture being presented, in the sense of how much what we are hearing about is predominantly culturally determined rather than a particular psychopathology of the family in question.

One simple example is that relating to play. In some cultures it is not usual for children and adults to play together. As a rule children play with each other while adults get on with their work or chores. It is not an expectation that mothers will play with their little ones, and they do not in a simple sense always know how to do this. A counsellor or other worker might be much more judgemental about the amount of attention being given to the child's play if this was not understood. On the other hand, in a family who has emigrated to this country, a child may nonetheless feel neglected and ignored by the parent. In the home culture the mother's approach was manageable and healthy in part because the extended family and teams of older siblings and cousins spent attentive time with the small child. However, this may well not be as tolerable in a small nuclear family where no-one else is around. In addition, the child's exposure through friends to other ways of parenting in British culture can affect the way in which he experiences it at home. The lack of playful contact may be very real, but its meaning will be different in that it will not stem so much from the parent's hostility or withdrawal from the child, more from a lack of awareness and lack of experience from which the parent could draw.

Knowing something about the culture of the family of our client can be invaluable in helping us ask the right questions but it can never provide the answers. In the psychodynamic way of thinking about child-care we would stress that it is often the underlying unconscious dynamics between a parent and a child that matter more than the actual child-rearing methods. It would be the meaning and the unconscious motivation for the parent in setting the boundaries around a child that might often matter more than the actual boundaries, within reason of course.

For instance, in mainstream British culture we expect children to sleep on their own at a very early age. This would be considered extremely odd and problematic in many cultures. However, a British mother making the decision to put the baby in a room of their own in a way would convey a very different set of meanings to the baby than if it were done by a Singalese mother, as the decision would be coming from a different place culturally and therefore have different psychological meaning. Conversely a British mother might be considered by some to be having difficulties in separating if a baby was breastfed for over a year or so, while in other cultures this would be completely unremarkable. Any assumption based on our own cultural practices is likely to be suspect and needs handling with care, but ignoring them completely might also mean that some important meaning is lost and faulty inferences drawn.

It is a continual tension for us to balance our own sense of what a child needs against the reality that the child has experienced with its specific meanings for the family. There is no neutral place to stand in this, and it is unhelpful to pretend that there is. All we can do is strive to clarify the meaning in this particular family of doing things the way they do, and the particular impact on this child of things being as they are, with an open mind as to how this is experienced. Keeping the child's own emotional experience as the central focus can provide us with a touchstone and can help us steer our thinking more effectively.

There may be aspects of cultural conflict that are completely explicit, but we need to be careful not to assume therefore that they are therefore simple. For example, Iranian Sara (16) complained bitterly to her counsellor about how she was not allowed out the way her school friends were, and that her fledgling relationship with a British boy was something she had to keep very secret in defiance of her strict father. Her way of talking about this would undoubtedly have been influenced by her assumption that being British her counsellor would be sympathetic to her view. If she had been talking to an Iranian counsellor she might have expressed herself differently as she would not have assumed that the counsellor would share her indignation. However, her British counsellor did not simply comply with her assumptions. She wondered out loud about how Sara imagined she would be listening to this, thinking maybe she would be expecting her unquestioning support. She wondered if Sara was trying inside herself to make it all simple, just her and the British (including her counsellor) against her old-fashioned father, so as to avoid any sense of conflict inside her.

Once this was aired, it was possible to explore with Sara her complex relationship with Iranian culture. She was struggling to make sense of it as a child growing up in a big English city, and in fact valued a lot of what made her family different, as well as fighting some of the constraints that went with this. She was caught between conflicting identifications and defensive manoeuvres. In one part of herself she despised some of what Britishness meant to her, in the other she despised some of what Iranian-ness meant to her. Before the counselling she had been bouncing uncomfortably and unthinkingly from one to another, but in the course of the counselling she could see that what she was fending off was the painful hard work needed to marry the two together, and to forge something of her own out of the conflicting demands of both. Once she was freed from having to take a simplistically polarized position in opposition to her father it was possible for her to have a much better discussion with him about the rules, to help him trust her and her friends a little more, and thence to have a more comfortable relationship with the boundaries around her.

## Racism

Anyone working with children (or adults) from a different culture needs to examine and confront their own prejudices and unconscious as well as conscious racism. The roots of racism run very deep, as is understood both in sociological and in psychodynamic theoretical approaches. In the psychodynamic framework, racism is predominantly seen as a response to our own fear and hatred of the Other, who can act as a repository for projections of the 'badness' in ourselves into someone recognizably different. Race is, as Rustin and Quagliata (1991) says, an 'empty category' into which anti-thought and psychotic mechanisms can be poured. We can split off all we disown in ourselves and hate and persecute it in the person who is different.

Racism is also fed by the weight of guilt and shame at damage done to the Other in our own and our culture's past. We fear those we have harmed, and we also fear those in whom we have evoked envy and retaliatory feelings. As a result someone from a race that has been abused in our colonial past, whose ancestors were so badly treated by our own, and from whose subjugation we indirectly have profited, can easily become feared. The fear can lead to a sense of persecution that brings hatred and hostility to the fore. Or we can respond with so much guilt – in psychoanalytic terms an overload of depressive anxiety – and this then leads to a failure of empathy and cutting off of emotional contact. Or it can lead to a falsity borne of compulsive and depersonalized reparation, robbing a real encounter of its personal truth. It can paralyse us as we fear repeating the abuse from the past so much that we cannot be effective in the face of aggression and destructiveness in our clients. Compulsive guilt and fear of being seen to be racist can lead to us not being able to look at the damage being done to our clients' own lives.

There are examples of this in the apparent reluctance of some workers to challenge parents from ethnic minorities who are neglecting or even abusing their children. In counselling it can easily take the form of not being as alert to or concerned about a family's way of doing things that is different from some (mythical) mainstream British way of doing things. If the child or adolescent we are working with presents a level of strictness or even physical punishment around them as the norm, and what is expected in the extended family, it can be difficult to ask the right questions about this without fearing that racism might be inferred.

Mai, a bright Japanese girl of 15, came to counselling because she was unhappy and falling behind in her work. She described a home in which the family's well-being was clearly valued over individual achievement or independence. She was unable to see a way forward for herself, and criticized herself endlessly for not making her father proud of her. When she got A's in her work she berated herself for not getting the A*'s her father expected and which would lead to the medical career that he had firmly in mind for her. The counsellor was well able to see the ways in which this girl's personal development was being inhibited by the conflict between her loyalty to the family and her resistance – even hostility – to her father, but felt unable to work effectively with her on this as she was filled with concern that she would be seen to be insensitive to the cultural norms in Japanese society. She felt that her British insistence on the importance of individual development rather than family concerns might be a racist stance, and so felt hampered in taking up Mai's internal conflict. In supervision it was possible to unpack this sufficiently for her to approach Mai with more confidence in following sessions. The counsellor was able to return to the work more able to respect that this conflict had a different flavour perhaps than it would for many a British girl, but still see it as something that could usefully be explored. Mai needed help in untangling her own wishes and needs, from her perspective within her own particular sense of her culture.

One aspect relating to difference that we have to be able to think about is the experiences of racism that children and adolescents from ethnic minorities will have experienced. It can be hard for anyone in the majority to know what it is like to be in a visibly different minority. White counsellors, even if they do not themselves feel as if they are mainstream, or even if they are not British and therefore themselves feel different, cannot truly know what it is like to walk down the road with friends with the knowledge that many of the people looking at them are unthinkingly casting them in the role of potential muggers, as is often the experience of black teenage boys. They cannot know fully what effect it has on these young men to be stopped and searched by the police over and over again, or to register people's surprise when they hear an educated voice or find out about an achievement. Mehmet (17) was able only after a long time to tell his counsellor of what it had meant to him to know that in his girlfriend's parents' eyes he was absolutely unacceptable. There was a triumph in his continuing to see her in the face of their opposition, but this was a thin blanket covering the humiliation at being automatically disqualified by the colour of his skin.

Racism can have immeasurably corrosive effects on one's self-image and self-esteem. This needs to be kept in mind when working with any child or adolescent in the consulting room, and if we are from a majority racial group we need to be alert to the likelihood that they will experience us as racist too. This extends to the family as well. The experience of witnessing racism towards parents will have had its effect on the child's image of his parents. Jackson (12) recalled seeing his father racially abused by a group of white men in the street. His father was diminished irrevocably in his son's eyes, even as the boy's anger against the white men was also aroused. Black children may react with a violent repudiation of the culture that routinely serves up humiliation and limits their prospects, and this can then seriously jeopardize their future and prevent them from making the best use of those around them who are trying to help. They may find it inherently more humiliating to accept help from a white counsellor, or even a black counsellor if she is identified with the prevailing culture.

Alternatively, they might internalize the racism that is all around them and secretly despise themselves for being black, or accept lower expectations of their achievements. They may unconsciously subscribe to a hatred of their own ethnicity. This can lead to small children trying to scrub off their blackness or in other ways attacking their skin. This dynamic can operate even within families, as in some Asian families a hierarchy of darkness of colour is a pronounced feature. This can mean that darker siblings feel themselves to be inferior. The meaning of the colour of one's skin is mutable and complex. One mixed race boy adopted into a white family often talked about 'wicked black' as a colour in his pictures. Blackness was associated in his mind with 'wickedness' – very much in both its senses. It was a badge of a defiant kind of superior merit but it was also an expression of a disposition to be on the 'bad' side.

We are expecting a very great deal of all the children we work with when we try to increase their hopefulness about themselves and to extend their emotional and practical potential. It is painful to move from states of mind where conflict is largely externalized to those where it is located more within (Dyke 1985). We are expecting even more if we are working with those who are socially and culturally disadvantaged. We will be working against the internal forces as with anyone, but also against external ones. Teachers may have lower expectations of these children, but the children may share this view. Tony (15) spoke of how all the boys like him are in prison or dead by the time they are 18. For Charlene (16) to aspire to go to university was to opt for what felt like a lonely life apart from her family and social circle. We can ourselves feel despair when faced with the way the odds are stacked against the children we work with. It is not easy to balance an awareness of the reality of the children's lives with a robust belief in their potential and a determination to help them make the most of themselves.

So far most of what has been written here has been from the point of view of a white counsellor, but there are other complexities involved if the counsellor herself is from an ethnic minority. Clients from the same ethnic group can act with a strong conscious or unconscious assumption of sameness (Davids 1998; Andreou 1999). This can possibly encourage easier early engagement, but can also set up very unhelpful emotional currents that undermine the effectiveness of the work, as confronting the client can be felt as a betrayal, or the counsellor can be seen as having sold out, become white, just by virtue of being a counsellor. There can be a racist assumption, even amongst those of a minority, that their counsellor cannot be as good if black. White British children can, perhaps even if they make conscious protestations to the contrary, struggle with their own racist assumptions that they are with a sub-standard counsellor, which may never be voiced. It there are racist attitudes at home, they may feel unable to trust or confide in a black counsellor. Even if there is nothing obviously negative in their attitude, their experience of the black counsellor will unavoidably be coloured by their assumptions and fantasies about racial difference, and it can be harder for them to open up with someone so obviously different.

For their part, a black counsellor may feel a range of difficult feelings towards a white client, including on occasion resentment and envy at their having so much easier access to certain kinds of success. It may feel more difficult to tackle issues of contempt and denigration if these feel linked to racial differences. Or the counsellor may be idealized and somewhat separated off from parental transferences because of her difference. It may also be harder for the counsellor to pick up on some transference communications because the differences seem to make them less available. A counsellor needs to have the courage to tackle these issues openly, as the client may never otherwise be able to explore the unconscious or semi-conscious dynamics that are obstructing the relationship.

Cultural assumptions of all kinds can be powerful in the room. If the counsellor has a foreign name, a strong accent or a darker complexion, there will be a change in the initial expectations of the client. These might perhaps be thought to be only larger, starker versions of what happens when the client sees a middle-aged rather than a young counsellor, or an overweight rather than a thin one. Each situation is going to bring with it emotional resonances for the client that will lead to particular perceptions of the counsellor's place in society in the light of which the counselling proceeds. But the unique power of racism, with its connection to the dynamics of power, issues of inferiority/superiority and insider/outsider-ness lends any ethnic difference a unique relevance in the relationship, which needs to be in the mind of the counsellor if it isn't to be an unconscious and unacknowledged corrosive element in the work.

## Differences in sexual orientation

Another kind of difference that is likely to be faced by the counsellor with young people is around sexuality. Even though Freud wrote repeatedly about our essentially bisexual nature, with all of us having homo- as well as heterosexual elements in us, until fairly recently there has been a tradition of pathologizing homosexuality in the psychoanalytic literature, with the prevailing idea that healthy development includes the establishment of heterosexual partnerships (see Bourne 2003, and responses from Taylor and McGuire 2003).

Working with adolescents who are just beginning their sexual explorations is bound to bring with it encounters with some who are finding themselves physically attracted to the same gender. It is also bound to bring work with those confused or troubled by their sexual orientation. Whatever our own sexual orientation, we need to have worked on our own attitudes sufficiently to be able to meet a troubled young man or woman with a suitably open mind and thoughtful capacity. Rather like with some aspects of the racial issue, what is most important is that we remain able to think, rather than be paralysed either by our own responses, or by our own fear of being seen to be prejudiced. In both these situations we will cease to be helpfully available to our client in thinking through what all this means to them.

It is obviously and crudely unhelpful and damaging if the counsellor acts or speaks as if the only healthy sexuality is heterosexuality and homosexual feelings are a sign of maladjustment. This may have been the approach of many psychoanalytic practitioners decades ago and is still to be found in some writers' work, but is not the prevailing way of thinking now (see Downey and Friedman 2008 for a discussion of recent developments in psychoanalytic thinking regarding homosexuality). However, even if a heterosexual counsellor consciously holds a theoretical view that allows homosexuality to be a full and valid expression of healthy sexual life, she may, as with racism, not have fully managed this in her inner world, or worked through the unconscious meaning of this for her in her own conflicts and anxieties around sexuality.

For example, Katie (16) came to counselling because she was involved in an intense feud with another girl who was calling her names, particularly teasing her about being a lesbian. Her tormentor was dealt with by the school in accordance with the policy on bullying, but it was felt that Katie could herself do with some help in managing this. It emerged in the counselling that she was in fact sure she was homosexual, and was quite happy with this. It wasn't being teased about this that worried her, but the way the other girl made out it was a bad thing to be. She spoke about having known about her sexual preference for ages, but interestingly she did not give the counsellor any indication of being actually attracted to another girl. It seemed to the counsellor to be more a self-chosen badge of defiance and difference, and that she was setting herself up to be bullied by her classmates by her rather provocative and masculine way of presenting herself. The counsellor took up the problems with this in mind, and the work foundered. As it only lasted a few sessions, it is hard to know precisely what was going on at a deeper level for Katie, but it is likely that one element in the failure to engage was the fact that the counsellor was not fully taking this girl's issues with her sexuality on board, and was too readily assuming that the homosexuality was not deeply founded. Interestingly, it would not have occurred to her that another client's heterosexuality was an assumed position.

This kind of problem is made much more complex by the likelihood that the whole area is extremely vexing for the client. They may well have their own internalized homophobia to deal with, as with internal racism, and may themselves feel that their sexuality is wrong and bad. The presenting problem may, to them, be their fears and anxieties about their sexuality, but to us it may be more a matter of having a harsh internal judge who is telling them they are wrong, particularly as their thinking about the 'right' way of being a sexual being is linked to their relationship with their parents. Our sexual lives are intimately bound up with our identifications with our parents, and with our conception of what couples are and how they work. Becoming sexual is often the cause of major internal conflicts, even if our own way of being, or imaging being a couple looks much the same from the outside as that of our parents. If that couple is very different then there will be elements at work that stir extremely complex and difficult feelings. As counsellors we need to be alert to the possibility that the choice of sexual object is bound up with these internalizations while at the same time not prejudging this to be necessarily the case. Desire is a hugely complex thing, and is affected by the storms and currents of our inner worlds, and changes in our inner worlds can lead to changes, to some extent, in whom we desire (O'Connor and Ryan 1993).

For example, Charlene (19) was heterosexual, and always attracted to (usually older) men who treated her badly. She came to counselling in despair of being able to establish a more stable relationship. As we explored the background to this it became clear that she was still very caught up in fantasy with her charismatic but wayward father whom she was internally always trying to 'win' from her mother whom he treated with contempt. The men she found irresistible were in many ways similar to him, and had the added attraction of being usually attached to someone else from whom she could seduce them. After much work on this, it was possible for her to become sexually interested in a very different kind of person, who in the past would have held no attractions for her, and conversely the older men ceased to have their hold on her. This opened up potential for making relationships with men who could offer her more. There was no longer the compulsive side to her attraction to them, which she missed, but on the other hand there was now scope for a different kind of connection, less driven but longer-lasting, to emerge. This is obviously an example of hetero- rather than homosexual desire, and most importantly not a change from one to another, but nonetheless it illustrates that desire can be influenced by internal changes, and is not, as it can often feel, in any overly simple sense hard-wired into our nature and totally sepa- rate from our relationship history.

Marta (13) found herself intensely attracted to an older girl who played in the same orchestra as she did. She admired her looks, counted the days until the next rehearsal and tried in every way to be near to and noticed by this girl. She came to counselling very uncomfortable about this, and worried that it meant she was gay. The counsellor felt in quite a dilemma. Should she help this girl feel more comfortable with her sexuality, and address the super-ego harshness that seemed so evident in her thinking, so that her feel- ings were no longer a matter of shame, or should she work to help the girl see that this was a normal 'crush', that had as like as not no bearing on how her adult sexuality would develop? As with racism, there can be a paralysis that sets in if we are so concerned with being 'correct' that we cannot allow the individual in front of us to show us what is going on for them. It would be harmful if the counsellor felt that there is a set agenda that she needs to follow around issues of sexuality, which would prevent an open-minded and sensitive exploration of the relationships, internal and external, that are being presented.

True sexual intimacy, whether homo- or heterosexual, is a diffi- cult and complex achievement, even for adults. For adolescents at the beginning of their sexual lives, it is even more fraught. Sexual activity of any kind can be used as a defence against, as well as an exploration of and development towards intimacy. It is the quality of the relationship and the underlying fantasies and anxieties about being open to and deeply engaged with another person that are what merits our closest attention, not the gender of the partner. Anti-intimate or exploitative sexual activity is damaging for an adolescent to be engaged in, whether this is homo- or heterosexual. It is this that requires our attention, rather than being preoccupied by the gender of the object. We may only too easily find ourselves taking up with a more questioning and judgemental attitude sexual activity if it is different from our own, and pick up negative aspects of it more readily. Or we might miss ways in which sexuality similar to our own is being used self-destructively. We are simply less likely to ask as deeply why a client is pursuing a particular course if it is the same as ours, as we may assume it must be healthy.

Alternatively a heterosexual counsellor may find it more difficult to take up promiscuous homosexuality for fear of being experienced as prejudiced. We know that there are particular, often acute, pressures in coping with homosexuality and the suspicion and hostility with which it is viewed by much of the world. This can in some cases lead to a different and more boundary-breaking attitude to sexual activity. As a result, as a heterosexual counsellor we may get confused and fearful about how to read it, and this might lead either to over-pathologizing or alternatively to a glossing over of self- or other-destructive behaviour.

Our sexual lives involve such complex dynamics around what Gianna Williams (1997a) calls 'self esteem and object esteem' and it is these that we need to attend to in our clients. Our sexual development involves negotiating intense and often anxious fantasies about the quality of and our relationships with our inner parents, about their sexual relationship and about our connections with other family members (Marie Zaphirou Woods 1988). It is a lifelong task for even the healthiest amongst us to find a way both to be at ease with the power of our sexual feelings as well as being able to stay in some control of how we express them and how much we let them rule our choices. Our sexual responses have their roots in deeply unconscious mechanisms that are linked to our earliest and most fundamental bodily and emotional experiences. It is beyond many adults to integrate their sexuality in the context of intimate and mutually fulfilling relationships. Helping adolescents with their beginnings in this part of their lives is always difficult, even if they let us try – which of course many do not. Embarrassment and shame about their sexuality, of whatever kind, can be intense at this time of their life, and difficulties are often defended against, either with bravado and acting out or by withdrawal. It can be hard to talk about these issues to anyone, let alone to an unrelated adult. Where there is a difference in sexuality between counsellor and client the scope for handling this delicate area clumsily is much greater (see Downey and Friedman 2008 for a fuller discussion of these issues).

## Differences in physical and intellectual ability

As a counsellor one might well be working with children or adolescents who have differences in their physical or intellectual ability, which could be mild or profound. As with the other differences described in this chapter, one of the first steps is for us as counsellors to acknowledge to ourselves and quite possibly to the children, that we cannot know what it is like to be them. It is the children's experience of their difficulties that matters, and what it means to them. We can still do something to help them find the best way forward, even if we can never share their experience.

We have to understand how hard it is to stay mentally healthy in the face of such difficulties. As Sinason (1992, p. 20) says, 'Opening your eyes ... to the realization that you will not be an Austen, Einsten, Madonna or Picasso can be painful enough to the ordinary adolescent. Opening your eyes to admitting you look, sound, walk, talk, move or think differently from the ordinary, average person, let alone a cult hero or heroine, takes greater reserves of courage, honesty and toleration of one's own envy.' As a defence against that envy and the huge anger at fate (or the parents as its representatives who have dealt you such a poor hand), there can develop an array of 'secondary handicaps' (Sinason op. cit.) that further diminish the child's prospects. These can take different forms, for example, playing the clown to get hurtful laughter more under one's control, the adoption of a 'smiling pet' role that cramps one's development, or the wilful diminution of one's actual abilities as part of the defensive cutting off to protect against pain. There could well be an undercurrent of anger and envy that can prevent enriching relationships, especially if it is denied and working unconsciously.

Helping a child get in touch with his feelings, which may often have been glossed over and denied by anxious, traumatized or guilty parents/carers, can be a painful but a potentially helpful experience. The emotional meaning and effects of the disability, of whatever kind, need full acknowledgement, but it can also help free up the child's potential to progress if we can look at ways in which he might be using it to hide from other painful conflicts. The envy and anger that can so cut the child off from others is going to have its role in the transference, and can be very usefully worked on in the room. This is not easy, as our own guilt about being healthy and able can get in the way, and the amount of emotional pain that we are exposing the children to can even seem unethical (Hoxter 1986). However, there is much to be gained through having someone engage with the actual felt reality of the children's condition, without the evasions, stereotyping and stigmatizing that is so often their experience.

In milder cases of intellectual impairment, it can be difficult to tell the difference between a difficulty in thinking and learning that is organically based and one that is emotional in origin (Chapter 6). There could be a danger that we might, with misplaced zeal, pursue an emotional agenda when the child is using his abilities as well as he can. Conversely we might miss the fact that there is trauma and emotional blockage behind the learning difficulty. It is not easy to keep an open mind as to what has caused the difficulties, and we need to be both sensitive to the child's abilities as well as alert to any signs in the work that there are defences reducing the child's capacity to use them. But equally we need to accept that there are many areas of a child's difficulties that maybe are beyond a counsellor's reach. We can assist any child to make the best of what they have got, and to help them come to some kind of accommodation with the fact that they may not be as bright or able as many of their contemporaries. Working with the inner worlds of those who have learning difficulties will help them reap emotional rewards, even if it may have no direct impact on their learning difficulties *per se*. It may not alleviate the underlying problem but it will help them move on in their lives and diminish the power of potentially destructive defensive structures and unconscious conflicts.

Each child comes to us with a unique combination of personal and cultural characteristics; some we will share and others will be markedly different from our own. Being able to acknowledge this to ourselves and, where useful, to the child, and being open to the nuances of what it means for them, will help us stay close to the emotional experience of the child and thereby help them make the best use of the resources available, both internal and external.

# 12

# WORKING IN DIFFERENT SETTINGS

Anyone working with children or adolescents will need to grasp the implications of working in their particular setting. Some understanding of the psychodynamics of the organizations and networks around both the child and the counsellor is vital as otherwise we will struggle to remain effective.

Each setting will have its own particular primary task, into which the counselling needs to fit. We need to recognize the relationships between the aims of the counselling and the overall aims of the organization, and be respectful of the differing priorities of the other professionals with whom we are working. Clarity about our role in relation to the roles of others, and an appreciation of the rivalries and conflicts inherent in organizational life can help us operate more helpfully and avoid taking personally matters that have their roots in institutional dynamics.

Institutions, as well as individuals, have an unconscious life, are prey to anxieties and evolve defences (see Obholzer 1994). These forces will be affecting the children, our colleagues and ourselves at all levels. An acute perception of them will help us read situations more accurately and avoid unhelpful enactments. Similarly the network of professionals around a particular child or family can become imbued with the dynamics of the case and re-enact them (Britton 1981). Workers resonate with the problems of their clients, and come under unconscious pressure to re-enact families' inner conflicts, and this can be played out across whole networks. The difficulties that the professionals have in working together can often be a result of family splits being played out between the different parts of the network, with the feelings that the child and family cannot deal with being passed around between the professionals.

As counsellors we will ourselves be part of this network and always need to have the potential for these dynamics in mind. We need to be attentive to our own role in relation to others, and there will also be times when we need to be active in helping the adults around the child to work better together. Understanding more about what can get in the way of productive cooperation will help us manage this better.

In the following two chapters I will look at some typical settings within which counsellors work with children and adolescents and isolate some of the key features that have an impact on the effectiveness of the work. Each setting will have its distinctive flavour and throw up particular challenges, opportunities, advantages and constraints.

# Schools

The most numerous providers of counselling for children and adolescents are schools. Until fairly recently this was concentrated almost entirely in secondary schools, but there are now many more projects starting up offering this kind of help in primary schools (e.g. Place to Be, Kids Company, A Space, The Durham Project, etc. see Barwick 2000). Whatever the age range, a school counsellor needs to be aware of a number of particular features of working in such a setting.

It is useful to think about the way in which the counselling relates to the overall task of the school. Schools may be seen as having a relatively simple remit to fulfil, of providing educational opportunities for the children, but their task has been widened to encompass emotional and behavioural aims and to embrace the welfare of the child more holistically (*Every Child Matters*, DfES 2003). This can be overwhelming for schools, and the confusion over the demands on them by society, as well as the conscious and unconscious burden of so much responsibility can cause schools real difficulties, which in turn can have a major impact on counselling provision. Anton Obholzer (1994, p. 171) once wrote of the Health Service that it was unconsciously assigned the role of the ' "keep death at bay" service'. Schools could be seen as increasingly expected to be a 'solve all our social and family problems service', a 'don't make us think about the impact of modern life on children service', a 'save us from feeling guilty about our parenting service', or more prosaically a 'keep children off the streets service'. Equally unrealistically, although maybe less corrosively, schools could be seen as a 'do away with inequalities service' or a 'make this a good country service'. Schools can in fact contribute a good deal to addressing all these tasks, but unconsciously the pressure to perform impossible duties can deeply interfere with the capacity of any organization to do what it can actually do well. A counsellor working in a school can play an important part in helping the school manage this, and a careful defining of our own role, with a respectful acknowledgement of all the different ingredients required to perform the varied tasks the school is performing, will go a long way in this.

There are many different ways a school counsellor might define their role, depending on the amount of time they have, their skills and interests and the brief allowed them by the school itself. Some school counsellors see their task as including the promotion of emotional development and emotional literacy throughout the school and therefore can be highly visible. They might work with groups, with staff, with parents, running workshops in classrooms and attending some school functions. Others regard their primary task more exclusively as offering individual counselling, and therefore are clear that some of these activities interfere too much with their capacity to do this effectively. Each counsellor needs to work out and have a shared understanding within the institution as to what might or might not be called for in their role. This can in turn help the school clarify how to use its different resources optimally and to work out what is possible, avoiding both defeatism and omnipotence.

Each school is likely to have, whether consciously articulated or not, a particular task they expect the counselling to perform. All will be wanting the children's emotional difficulties to be addressed and for fuller functioning to be restored. However, there are many variations on this. Some may see counselling as primarily anger management, some may want educational blocks removed, and some may want children to be made more able to conform. At a less conscious level, some may want a way of protecting teachers from their sense of failure with difficult children, to permit the other staff not to attend to the children's emotional pain, or to provide respite from the most disruptive from the class. There are numerous other possibilities, but what is important is that we try to tune into the dynamics around the counselling in order to provide an effective service and avoid the many inter-professional impasses that can arise from such unconscious forces.

In terms of the clinical work, the most powerful advantage for a counsellor in a school is that the children are, on the whole, physically present. They do not need to be brought especially to the counselling, and they are, as a result, much more likely to attend and to attend regularly. Consistent parental involvement is not required, which is both an advantage and a disadvantage (Chapter 9). It is possible, if working in a school, to create an atmosphere around the counselling that reduces the anxiety and stigma that can be attached to seeking this kind of help, and to present counselling as a normal resource available in the school for pupils who are having a difficult time. It is relatively easy for a child to be referred, and this means that less dramatically needy children can be catered for, at an early stage of the development of their difficulties rather than when all else has failed or when anxieties have been raised all around them.

The counselling is near at hand, and this makes it easier for a child perhaps to have a period of counselling, finish and then return if something more is needed, without the drama and urgency implied by a referral or re-referral to an outside agency. Very importantly, attendance is much more likely to be maintained, partly as it takes so much less effort to come, but also because the counselling is felt to be part of the school's provision and is therefore less threatening. If the counselling is supported by the school, then encouragement from teachers and other important adults in the child's life can strengthen the elements in the child that want help against whatever internal forces there may be that make this hard. There is less likelihood of outside influences sabotaging or rendering more difficult their engagement and as a result their resistances are less likely to overwhelm their wish for change. Counselling being integrated into the overall developmental task of the school can make it easier for the children to get emotional help as they can come without feeling as if they have come unstuck to the extent they might if referred to another agency more identified with illness or with breakdown.

There are also some disadvantages, and particular features that need careful attention. Schools are usually very busy and pressured places, often without any spare time or space. This can lead to practical threats to the stability of the counselling provision, commonly for example if the room is required for other purposes. One familiar experience is for the room to be used for something else when the counsellor is not in, such as special reading help or medical examinations, or for meetings with parents. This will colour the child's experience of the room. In other cases the room is respected most of the year, but at examination times required for special events such as language oral tests. So the room can often not be kept as dedicated as the counsellor might like.

As schools operate relatively short terms, with half-term holidays, there is rarely a stretch of more than six sessions without a break. Furthermore, sessions are often disrupted by school trips, exams, assemblies, etc. As a result, school sessions are rarely going to have the continuity and dependability that psychotherapists in health service settings tend to count on in their work. This will need to be worked with all the time, and will affect the transference with all the children. It will especially make it more difficult to reach children for whom continuity and dependability are essential for them to take the risk of opening up and those whose home lives are currently reinforcing the need for defences.

Teachers are naturally primarily concerned with the academic work of the children, and this may mean that for the child to take time out of lessons is difficult for the teachers to endorse. Such concerns, especially in secondary schools, can mean that sessions have to rotate through the timetable to avoid missing too many of the same lesson. The consequence of this is that we have to forego another element of the therapeutic 'frame' highly valued in clinic work, that of always having a session at the same time on the same day. (For more on the therapeutic frame, see Copley and Forryan 1987; Gray 1994; Hartnup in Lanyado and Horne 1999.) As made clear by Music and Hall (2008, p. 49), a school counsellor has to 'rely on having inside us a safe and dependable internal frame ... something that in pressured moments is beyond even the most experienced therapist.'

There are other practical issues that can make a school counsellor's life complex. There will have to be some agreed method of getting the children from classroom to counselling room and back again. This latter can be a difficult issue, as collecting children from the classroom (often the usual practice in primary schools) gives both child and counsellor the challenge of managing the transition. It can throw up awkward moments, for example if the child is being told off by the teacher as the counsellor appears, or if the teacher hands the child over with a complaint to the counsellor about how he has been behaving or with a manner that implies that the counselling is a fun treat. The stage is set at such moments for acting out on all sides, with potential for the teacher to demonstrate any fantasies or difficulties they have with the counselling or the child, to confront their feelings about the counselling, and potentially set up difficult dynamics between the teacher and counsellor.

In a secondary school, it may be expected, especially with the older children, that they will manage their sessions themselves. However, there will need to be a system to notify teachers that they will be absent from lessons, and children can need reminding. In one school, there was a system by which, if a child did not attend as expected, a secretary went to get them, so that they could be extracted from class discreetly without it being obvious that they were going to counselling. This worked well most of the time, with it only being used occasionally and usually when a child was in a double lesson and had not been aware of the time. However, one child was always 'forgetting' as she was very resistant to the work (which was paralleled by a serious truancy problem) and the secretary became understandably annoyed at having to spend so much time away from her desk. The system was abandoned for one where the children were expected always to find their own way, which meant an easing of adult relationships but brought with it an increase in lateness and 'no shows', some from children who were otherwise making good use of the counselling. There is no right way to manage these logistical difficulties, but they are always going to be part of what a school counsellor has to negotiate in order for her role to be viable.

Moving beyond the practical issues, schools in general and/or individual teachers may not be supportive of the counselling and may sometimes explicitly and consciously make their disagreements felt. Perhaps even more problematically, they may also unconsciously sabotage the provision by making it difficult for the child to attend regularly or by repeatedly unsettling the setting. This could take the form of interrupting sessions, keeping children late, or talking to the counsellor about the child's difficulties in an unboundaried way when the child is present. As counsellors we can be the objects of envy, having one child at a time for quiet and concentrated attention, which for most teachers is an unimaginable luxury. We can also be viewed with contempt, offering something so nebulous and apparently indulgent, when teacher feels that what the child needs is more discipline or to be excluded. It is possible for teachers to feel threatened by us, who, they might feel, are assessing them both in their work and in their mental health and are seeing their difficulties. We can become the focus of a range of projections, some helpful and some unhelpful, and this can and will have a major effect on the provision (see Barwick 2000; Music and Hall 2008).

For children and counsellors, there is a public quality to the counselling in a school that brings both positive and negative consequences. As already stated, counselling, being a publicly visible and acknowledged provision, can usefully lessen the stigma as it is being offered as a normal part of pastoral care. Children can recommend the counselling to one another and help friends about whom they are worried take the plunge into self-referral. They can see others being helped by it and be reassured about counselling from how they see others react. From our point of view it can also be very helpful to have a sense of how the child is managing himself in school, and to have accessible information about whether the child is functioning better or not as the counselling proceeds.

However, this public quality brings its own problems as well. We have to take account of how the child may feel seeing us around the school when not available to them, and to register what it means for the child to know some of the other children that we are seeing. If we are working with a child who is perceived by others to be 'weird', 'crazy' or 'dumb', then that could put off some children with difficulties, as they do not want to be associated with that kind of child. If we are seeing or have seen someone with whom a child has a difficult relationship, they may not feel confident that we can be trusted and are not already biased against them. The children can discuss us and the counselling together, which can disrupt the way in which a piece of work may go, or the rivalry between the children can make it difficult for them to make best use of the work. For those children for whom sibling rivalry has been overwhelming it can be too difficult to see a counsellor who is so obviously and manifestly shared by others.

On another level, the more public we are as a person in the school the less neutral our image will be, and while this may help some children come to and use the counselling it may also keep others away. It certainly means that there will be a more defined sense of who we actually are, which will have its effect on how easily a transference that is particular to this individual child can be established and clarified.

For some children their need for privacy may mean that shared counselling cannot work. They may feel too much shame about their difficulty to be able to manage bringing it to counselling in a school setting or risk being seen to need help by their peers in a way that will jeopardize their standing in the school. They may not be able to lower their defences enough in school to be able to open up to the counsellor. They know that they have to leave the counselling room and return to class, often without much space to recover from upsetting feelings and to organize themselves to be ready for communal life. Many children in major difficulties cope with school by keeping home distress rigidly compartmentalized, and may feel therefore that their capacity to function well in school may be jeopardized by getting in touch with painful feelings when in a place that is being kept relatively insulated from them.

For teenagers particularly, the last thing some may want is to have their private intimate business aired in school. However much confidentiality is assured, they may not be able to trust the counsellor enough to put this terror aside and make use of the work. They may fear information becoming available to teachers or their families more than they would if they were seeking help in a separate agency. They may associate school with humiliation and belittlement in a way that will make the idea of counselling in school an anathema. As a school counsellor, although not a teacher, we may be too close in their minds to being a teacher to be trusted, let alone for there to be a real hope of being understood. Adolescents are often able to cope with difficulties by using major splits between what can feel like separate versions of themselves, and to bring school and their personal emotional conflicts together may seem too difficult or unmanageable. For these clients an out of school provision is going to work better.

Teachers may understandably want pupils' problems to be solved quickly and the shared space of the school may lead to them showing their disappointment at slow progress in an open denigration of the counselling. The expectations of the school can weigh heavily on us. We may have our own sense of the child being strongly engaged in the work but feel pressured by this not yet bearing fruit in the school setting. If we were working outside we could probably withstand this more comfortably and be more able to keep our own sense of the progress of the work free from outside influence. On the other hand, it is useful to be aware if an apparently good alliance in the counselling is manifestly not making for tangible change in the rest of the child's life. This need not be taken as signifying that the counselling is simply not working. More time may be needed before progress is likely to show, and it is also the case that in some instances problems may become temporarily more acute as conflicts become more accessible. However, it can also mean that there is a split that needs attention and that a one-to-one relationship is being idealized at the expense of something else in the system.

For example, one counsellor became frustrated at the school's lack of understanding of Seymour (9), who was, after a difficult start, working very well and cooperatively in the room. He was charming and playful, seemingly working hard in his use of the toy animals and art materials. She felt he was letting her into his inner emotional world and allowing her to think about his difficult home life. Outside the room Seymour's propensity to get into fights and to be aggressive with other children and defiant with teachers was undiminished. While the progress in the room was not an illusion, it was far from the whole story. It was not a simple matter of the counsellor understanding the child and the school not, which was sometimes how she felt. It was vital that she could hold in mind that the charming boy she saw was also the violent child the teaching staff saw, and to help him pull these parts of him together. It was actively unhelpful for her to collude in the splitting, in which he was showing his good side for her to see but the bad side was being strenuously kept out of the counselling.

However, there is another difficulty here, which is how to integrate information that we might be aware of that is not brought by the child themselves. The counsellor in this case felt very uncomfortable about the risk of ruining her good relationship with Seymour by letting him know that she knew he had been in trouble for fighting. It also meant introducing information into the sessions that she had received from other sources, which is always awkward and often to be discouraged. It required skillful commentary and interpretations to help him see that she was aware that he was only showing her the nicest parts of himself. She observed, when appropriate, that she could see how important he felt it was to keep everything nice in the room. She would mention that he was protecting both her and himself from anything difficult arising, creating a lovely 'I'm nice, you're nice' twosome, when this was perhaps likely not to be the whole story. She knew he was not doing this in a simple way to deceive, he needed a good relationship, but he was also keeping at bay his terror that he would be rejected if he showed his bad side in the room. She could therefore speak to him about how much he needed it to be nice in the counselling room because he was so afraid it could all get spoiled otherwise. He was, however, not helping himself in the long run, and with her help he was able to bring more of the difficulty into the room and begin more engaged work on the issues that went wrong for him outside.

Another counsellor was alerted by staff that much of what she was learning from Mina (14) was untrue. This was deeply disturbing, although potentially also very useful information. The counsellor felt paralysed by it, as she felt duped and rendered stupid if she went along with the stories, but feared she would lose what connection she had with Mina if she let on that she no longer believed her. She tried to adapt her way of listening to make room for the possibility that it was not all true, but Mina picked up the change quickly, became defensive and left the counselling. One could argue that the counselling was being misused, and was not likely to lead anywhere if Mina was falsifying so much. However, if the counsellor had not learned about the deceptions and the work had continued, it is possible that sufficient emotional work could have been done for a more honest relationship to emerge. As it was, the relationship could not survive the intrusion from outside knowledge and foundered.

This is not to say in any simple way that it is better not to know when one is being misled, or that a counsellor should be insulated from the knowledge that the school has of the child, far from it. However, it needs to be acknowledged how difficult it can be to handle such information. Knowing too much can prevent one encountering the child as he is now, with us, and creating a unique relationship with them that is not overly affected by the views of others, but knowing too little can mean that we are hampered in our ability to tune in usefully to what is really going on. There is no simple way of resolving this tension, but one of the skills required of a school-based counsellor is to manage it as creatively as possible whilst acknowledging its inherent difficulty. If we know a lot we still have to free our minds enough to find our own way to the child and to encounter his emotional reality. If we know very little we have to manage a good deal of uncertainty and lack of context that can make reading the child's communications more difficult.

Another aspect of the public quality of school counselling is that our standing in the child's eyes is also likely to be affected by the way we are regarded by the school. If we are respected and the child has good feelings about the school, this will be benign, but this will not always be the case. For example, in one school where a counsellor had been working for over a year, she was still stopped by staff in the corridor and asked who she was, sometimes in front of a child she was working with. This, and other similar illustrations of our status, is bound to have its effect on the transference. This can work in another way as well, with our maybe being seen by the child to be on friendly terms with teachers about whom the child has difficult feelings, and this can then play its own part in making it harder for the child to use us freely.

Furthermore, as indicated above regarding Seymour, there is

significant scope for the child also to make unhelpful splits between us as the counsellor and the teachers. The following example is more from the point of view of the pressure on the counsellor in our role in relation to other staff. There will be a different quality to the interaction if a child is complaining about a teacher's unfairness or meanness to us as a school counsellor, as opposed to one outside the school, as we can reasonably be expected to know the teacher in question. The child can try to exert pressure on us to become their champion, in a way that is less likely with an external counsellor. If a child is felt to be being treated unfairly by the teaching staff, it can at times be hard for us to work out how best to remain in the role. The child can misuse the counselling as a reason to avoid work, or as an excuse for missing lessons. The child can exert pressure on us to be the 'good guy' at the expense of the teacher, and this can be a seduction that we may not always manage to avoid. We always have to be vigilant about these dynamics, and be alert to the ways in which we are being used by the child in the overall picture of his school life, more than would be called for in work with an external counsellor.

For example, John (14) complained bitterly to his counsellor about the unfairness of several teachers. She was given a highly convincing picture of his being picked on and punished for transgressions that other children were allowed to get away with. She felt considerable pressure to intervene on his behalf and to speak to the teachers, especially when detentions and exclusions began to threaten the counselling. John never seemed at all difficult with her, and seemed to value her input. She had her own feelings about the strictness of the school and its relative lack of emotional literacy, and this exerted its own pressure on her to see John as the victim of an unfair and unsympathetic system.

However, as she worked to resist the temptation to take up cudgels on his behalf, she began to explore more deeply with him about what all this meant and where it fitted into a larger picture. It began to become clear that, much as he hated always being in trouble, the idea of not being so was problematic as well. He had a certain prestige in the school as a result of his being punished often, and he had (defensive) contempt for children who were 'nerds' and 'boffins'. He was contemptuous of the teachers and this linked to contempt for his parents. His mother was borderline alcoholic and had given up trying to set limits on his behaviour or going out. His father had left home when he was 7 years old after violent scenes.

Underneath the picked-on victim was a very troubled young man with several layers of difficulty. He was yearning for proper parenting, while at the same time compelled by his infantile anger with inadequate adults to defy and provoke. The sense of unfairness was by no means confined to school, but was the pervading emotion of his life, and had become built in to his idea of himself. However uncomfortable it was, it gave a shape to the deep sense of grievance that dominated his internal landscape, and it was almost as if he would not have known what to do with a kind or attentive teacher. Unconsciously he set about setting the teachers against him, by subtle and not so subtle provocation. He idealized the counsellor to keep her safe from his disappointment and rage, but at the same time risked making her also impotent to help him by enacting a split that would have been fruitless and anti-therapeutic.

His vulnerable and needy self was protected from view by others and from his own contempt and fear by the constant state of indignation at the blatant unfairness of the world. This is a very different emotion from longing or sadness, and protected him from his own need to learn or to create a good relationship with someone. If the counsellor had just been on his side she would never have been able to explore these deeper areas and help to release him from the destructive cycle he was caught in.

This example highlights the possibilities for splitting in school work, but there are ways in which the embeddedness of the counsellor can be used more actively and fruitfully.

Karina (16) was seen by teaching staff to be quiet but able, and to be managing extremely well. The counsellor was aware that underneath this surface she was extremely depressed and in fact struggling to keep going, with suicidal thoughts sometimes overtaking her. It was possible for the counsellor (with Karina's consent) to speak to the head of year and to alert her to how overwhelmed Karina could be. This was a surprise to the teaching staff concerned, as Karina hid her distress effectively, but led to much more sensitive handling of this vulnerable girl.

Perry (8) was being seen by the counsellor in his primary school, referred as he was withdrawn and being bullied by some older boys. The counsellor became aware of how hard it was for Perry to feel he truly had a right to claim a place in the world as a result of his mother's preoccupation with an older brother who had died. Without having to share the details with the teacher, she worked with the teacher over giving Perry responsible roles in the class and helping him gently via class activities to encounter his more competitive feelings. Sharing her understanding of Perry's conflicted feelings the counsellor helped the teacher be more active herself in bringing him out of himself, which she had hitherto been too uncertain and anxious to do. Florence Heller (in Barwick 2000) brings out several similar examples in which the active but careful collaboration between counsellor and teaching staff can have strongly positive results.

The child's experience of adults working constructively together on his or her behalf can have a major impact, both in terms of what it can bring about – a more constructive meeting, a stronger integration of parts of the self, a better understanding on both sides – but also as a representative of the capacity of adults to combine efforts in a positive way, something that the children have so often lacked in terms of their family experiences. Where counsellor and school are in a good enough relationship, there can be a powerful reinforcement of the efficacy of effort on both sides, with the child able to benefit from the improved holding offered by this metaphorical couple.

# 13

# FAMILY CONSULTATION CENTRES, COMMUNITY ADOLESCENT SERVICES AND BEYOND

## Child and adolescent mental health services/family consultation centres

A counsellor or other professional offering counselling in a Child and Family Consultation Centre is in a different position from one in a school. As part of the multi-disciplinary provision the counselling would be one of a wide range of interventions available to families. Children are likely to have an assessment as a separate venture, often by other professionals, and then referred to counselling where this is seen as appropriate. The counsellor is therefore not the front-line provider as in a school, so we may have more control over the referral criteria and be more active in the thinking about which kind of cases are taken on. Mental health and psychological treatment are the core preoccupations of the agency, unlike in a school, and so the counselling is situated very differently within the agency and in relation to its primary task.

The experience for the child is different from being seen in school. Being referred to an outside clinic is likely to feel a more major event than going to a school counsellor. There may be more hope that in this different setting the adults will also be different from the other adults the child has encountered. This may give the child a stronger sense that his difficulties are being taken seriously and that expert help is at hand. On the other hand, referral to a Child and Family Consultation Centres may feel more stigmatizing and raise greater anxieties about mental illness and madness. There will be more of a doctor than a teacher quality to the pre-transference which may on the one hand make the counsellor more effective and less punitive but on the other may mean that they are thought to be powerful and more frightening in the child's mind.

Going to a Child and Family Consultation Centre with one's family is a different experience from visiting a counsellor on one's own in school time. The shared experience of getting help with the family, taking its own part in the search for improvement, can be a liberating and hopeful experience for the child. One extremely helpful aspect of seeing children in a Child and Family Consultation Centre is that one is not tied to school terms, so that the periods of unbroken attendance can be much longer, and the breaks much shorter. This can be invaluable for more vulnerable children, who may not be able to manage to hold onto the work during the long and frequent breaks in school-based work. On the other hand, clinic attendance can actually be more erratic than in schools. Troubled and anxious families may be resistant to the work and attend irregularly, and escort arrangements for children without attending families can break down easily. If families are attending together, the risks that one or other member will be busy, ill or reluctant and find a reason for not attending are higher as more people are involved. Families referred to Child and Family Consultation Centres are by definition likely to have complex needs and therefore are perhaps more likely to be chaotic or to feel persecuted enough to make regular attendance a great challenge.

Working in a Child and Family Consultation Centre brings with it both the unique opportunities and the complexities of working in a multidisciplinary team. In any given service there will be multiple professions with a variety of trainings, each likely to believe strongly in their model of work. We may need to be able to defend psychodynamic and individual work against the doubts and scepticism of those trained differently. As counsellors we are likely to be a relatively junior member of the team, which can bring difficulties and challenge our capacity to own our full authority in the role. However, an advantage is that we are in a position to be able to learn about other approaches and see where and when other kinds of work are preferentially indicated. This can confirm the unique contribution of all the disciplines, including a strong sense of where and when counselling is the treatment of choice. In a well-resourced and well-functioning team we may be able to call on multi-disciplinary support for the case and fruitful collaboration between different professions. Some children can make good use of a range of different professionals. In some services there will be scope for family work prior to and/or alongside individual counselling or there can be psychiatric or social work support to complement the counselling (see Chapter 15 on Assessment).

For example, Sinitta (17) was a depressed, overweight teenager who saw her counsellor weekly but also saw a psychiatrist every six weeks to monitor her medication and to oversee the medical aspects of her progress. Her mother was seeing a social worker within the team every two weeks, and every term the whole family came for a meeting. The work with mother concentrated on lessening the enmeshment between mother and daughter, as mother was finding it hard to let Sinitta grow up. Work with Sinitta focused on getting in touch with her anger and confusion about her father who was living abroad, and her difficulties in letting herself fully move on into adult life. This collaboration worked well, and each element was essential for the eventual good outcome.

An example of a more complex case would be Irene (6), who was referred by a speech therapist as she was not speaking at school. She was withdrawn and not interested in learning. An assessment took place including Irene's mother and new partner. There was a complex family situation revealed in the meeting, which included the fact that Irene had been left with relatives in the Philippines while her mother came to the UK to work. She kept in touch but when she returned five years later she found Irene was not being well treated and brought her back with her to the UK. The assessment led to Irene being taken on for weekly counselling, while her mother was offered her own fortnightly meetings.

Irene presented in counselling as a very anxious child, barely holding herself together and constantly on guard. She gave the counsellor a vivid version of her own abandonment by playing in a way that left the counsellor shut out and excluded. No verbal communication took place, and the counsellor felt punished, perhaps giving an emotional clue to a component of the motivation behind the non-speaking.

In the work with the clinic social worker the mother was able to put into words how hurt and helpless she felt in relation to Irene's refusal to talk to her. She was helped to think about her daughter's experience of the separation and slowly became able to manage the guilt she felt. This enabled her gradually to gain enough courage to get more in touch with Irene's feelings, and their engagement became more real and attuned.

The counselling with Irene continued, with an emphasis on games that had the quality of reworking very early dynamics. The counsellor often had to take up the stance of a mother with an infant, having to be acutely attuned to non-verbally expressed needs and becoming adept at guessing what she wanted. In the play and relationship with her counsellor Irene was also able to get very angry and express fury that had its roots in her feelings about those who had mistreated her, and this helped unblock some of the inhibitions behind her withdrawal.

Interestingly, Irene never spoke in counselling, but six months later was talking at school and at home, was much more engaged in learning and was generally felt to be doing well. Both mother and daughter were happier, and their relationship much improved. It is likely that there would have been much less chance of a good outcome if help had been offered to Irene without help for her mother, or alternatively to the mother without help for her daughter, as there was important work to be done on both sides for the relationship to be re-established and her development resumed.

Effective collaboration like this takes a great deal of work and mutual respect. It is also expensive, and a key difficulty in such work can be the pressure on resources. In general, Child and Family Consultation Centre teams are more likely than school counselling services to be under intense scrutiny as to throughput and waiting list delay times. On the one hand they can offer the possibility of longer-term and more intensive work with children and families, whether with the counsellor or other professionals such as a psychotherapist, but if resources are tight we may not have much freedom as to how, for how long or how intensively we can see a child. We may have to refine and develop our ability to work short-term (Chapter 14) or adapt our techniques to fit treatment plans dictated by other professionals. We have to define much more sharply what it is about psychodynamic counselling that is different and uniquely valuable, as it is only one of many possible interventions – and outcomes are measured more rigorously than is usual in educational settings.

It might be assumed that, Child and Family Consultation Centre being a specialist service, the children referred there would be likely on average to be more disturbed and have more complex difficulties. To a large extent this will be true, but it is not a given. In school and community work we have to be able to at least assess all comers, some of whom may be very disturbed indeed, without prior screening. As Music and Hall (2008, p. 49) say, 'In fact, often it is the most complex cases (the cases that professionals are most desperate about), which might never make it to a clinic, which are referred in school.' In a school therefore, we need to be acutely tuned to the level of disturbance (Chapter 12). Being the only psychological professional in a school may leave us much more open to unexpected developments. In addition, while in a school we may well be seeing children with far less in the way of family or network support. In a Child and Family Consultation Centre, by definition, someone has noticed the child's distress or problematic behaviour enough to refer, and someone has taken enough trouble to bring the child for help. There are other colleagues with whom the assessment experience can be shared and there is the possibility of co-working during both assessment and treatment.

When specialist mental health intervention is required, then a referral to a Child and Family Consultation Centre may need to be the next step. As a result, those offering counselling within a Child and Family Consultation Centre are in general likely to be dealing with much deeper and more complex psychopathology, and may therefore need to work at a deeper and more subtle level. This is also made more possible by the setting. The children will be able to experience us more as an outside person in their lives, which greatly frees up the possibilities in terms of transference work, as we can retain more anonymity and separateness. Much more can be left in the realm of the children's fantasies about us (e.g. the other children who attend) and they will not have to deal with seeing us around when not available to them. Our insight into their inner worlds will be made more direct as they know less about us. This makes possible a deeper and more infantile transference closer to that fostered in psychotherapy, and therefore has the potential to address deeper levels of disturbance.

## Community-based services

Community-based services, particularly likely to be a setting for adolescent work, occupy a different but related territory. They are naturally less likely to provoke a pre-transference influenced by ideas about doctors or mental illness. Attendance at such a service is usually more voluntary for the adolescent, and may even be run primarily on a self-referral or drop-in basis. This has the advantage that the adolescent has already been able to admit he needs help in order to come, and has personally made the move to access it. He has made more of an individual decision to be there than if sent to a clinic or a school counsellor, and the work is more likely to be felt by them to be truly theirs.

Nonetheless, there are still difficulties in such an agency around engaging the young person, as there may be little support structure to help them become and stay committed to the work. The parents may well not know that the adolescent is seeking help, and this itself can create difficulties for the counsellor (see Chapter 10 on Consent). It is a central and ongoing task of the counselling therefore to maintain engagement. This requires skilful footwork and particularly a readiness to take up the transference and internal world issues, as the external life of the adolescent is so much more at a distance.

Moreover, there is an even more pressing need to take up any negative aspects in the work in the room. We can so easily lose a client if he is trying to let us know about his difficult self, his destructiveness and contempt, and we do not realize fully or quickly enough that these are alive in the work itself (Temperley 1979). Working so much more completely on our own, we need even more urgently to collect all the parts of the client's personality into the work, or there is a risk that he will disengage. With so much less holding him there, we need paradoxically to be extra careful not to be collusive or seductive but to be alert to the nuances of how the client relates to us as the key to the work (see Mak-Pearce in Baruch 2001).

For example, Mario (17) referred himself to a drop-in adolescent service because he had been told he needed to get help as his college course was at risk and he did not want to seek help from the college support services. He was persistently late in completing assignments. When he came for counselling he gave enormously persuasive reasons for this; he had a part-time job, had to help out a lot at home, and had a long journey that ate up a lot of his time. The counsellor at first felt very sympathetic, impressed that this young man was managing as much as he was. She admired his apparent openness and felt annoyed with the college for being so strict and his mother for expecting so much from him. It was hard for her to spot the subtle way in which he was recruiting her onto his 'side' and creating an idealized togetherness. However, after a week's break occasioned by her having a prior commitment he began to miss sessions, with extremely plausible reasons given each time. She was then able to take up his ambivalence, and managed then to start work on his powerful defences against dependence and learning. His growing up was being stalled by, among other things, resentful feelings about his mother's new relationship, after a long period in which he had felt he had her to himself. The missed week had awakened (albeit unconsciously) his anger with a mother who pursued her own life and was not under his control, and this brought to the surface some key dynamics in his resistance to moving on with his work and to his tutor.

Mario was at risk of spoiling his educational progress, but not in other ways posing a serious risk to himself. However, in a community setting such as this, a first and continuing task as such is going to be risk-assessment. We need on an ongoing basis to be making a judgement as to the adolescent's degree of risk of suicide, self-harm or other self-destructive behaviour or risk-seeking tendency. The adolescent is not openly involved with other professionals who can share the concern and also be attending to their welfare, so the onus is more on us as the counsellor. We need to be even more alert than anywhere else to the moments at which we might need to inform or engage others in the care of the client. Some may approach the agency and be offered counselling when they lack sufficient support in the real world and may not have the stability in their outside life that would make inner world exploration a safe enterprise. This needs to be carefully assessed (see Chapter 15 on Assessment) and monitored as otherwise the work could potentially put them more at risk.

Regarding the transference, in a community service we have the same advantage as in a clinic, in that we can work relatively unencumbered by a link with the young person's other settings. The young person does not know anything more about us than what he can glean directly, and we are independent of all the other structures around him in his external life. This can give us a great freedom to explore his inner world. We will still be subject to a probable setting-dependent pre-transference. This might typically lead to the adolescent, like Mario, thinking that in such a service people are more likely 'on his side' or more in tune with young people. This may initially be potentially positive, but nonetheless will need to be worked with in order for the negative to come through and make itself available for attention.

Counsellors in such agencies may well be just one of a number of services available to the clients. There might be housing, employment, legal, health and other advice offered by the same agency, with counselling a small part of the overall operation. Again this has advantages and disadvantages. We can be perceived as part of more general assistance with a difficult stage of life and an acceptable resource alongside more practical input. We can have colleagues who, while primarily helping the adolescents with other aspects of their lives, can spot who could be helped by counselling and refer them in an unthreatening way. We can do our particular job, while others are helping the young people to get access to more practical advice and support where needed. This can help free us to work appropriately, which might be difficult if such other services were not available. For example, David (18) was an unaccompanied refugee who was able to access counselling to tackle his isolation and depression, while also getting help with his benefit and housing situation. Counselling alone would not have been appropriate, as there was so much of a practical nature that he needed help with as well.

There can, however, also be difficulties in such a setting. The atmosphere in such an agency can be dominated by the other approaches, and it can be hard to protect the quieter and more private provision of counselling. Other workers may identify much more openly with the adolescents as they begin to steer their way in the adult world. This can make it difficult, both for the client to explore their more child-selves and for us as counsellors to take up more difficult parental transferences. There can be conflict between adults offering different services as each sees the young person as being their client. Practical solutions to problems can be seen as being more relevant than work on their inner worlds. If the young person voices any reluctance to come to counselling, other workers are well placed to steer the child back, but may understandably, but perhaps too easily, suggest stopping or offer something else, rather than help them work through whatever may be difficult. There needs to be a lot of work done organizationally to help work on such problems, but the structure of such agencies can at times be much looser, with part-time workers from a range of employers under one roof, each with their own priorities and making multi-disciplinary working harder to encourage and support.

## Medical Settings

### GP practices

If employed as a counsellor in a GP practice we will most likely be working with children or adolescents whose problems are being made manifest in a bodily way whether this is psychosomatic illness, sleeping disturbances, eating disorders or self-harm. However, referrals could also frequently include young people with depression and in some cases those with family relationship difficulties, as the GP is often the first port of call for families who are concerned and do not know where else to turn. The particular types of cases most likely to be met in such a setting will require a greater level of understanding of how the emotional and physical interrelate (McDougall 1989; Turp 2002). In addition, we might be referring children who have a clearly organic illness but who are seen to need some emotional help in dealing with the impact of this on their lives (Judd 1989; Dale in Szur and Miller 1991).

The counselling experience in such a setting will have its own particular flavour, both for us and for the child. He will bring a pre-transference coloured by the medical setting, and is more likely to be expecting a diagnosis and moreover a treatment or cure in the form of medication or instruction. He is, as a result, perhaps likely to come with a more passive sense of his role in his problem. He will need to be actively enrolled in his own treatment before it is likely to work (see Chapter 10 on Consent). He may resist a psychological view of his difficulties, particularly if the symptoms are chiefly physical. The medical model will be a powerful part of the atmosphere around the work, even if the client has agreed to counselling and thereby consented in some way to psychological intervention.

From our point of view the setting will exert its own pressures on the work. Often GP practices stipulate a limited number of sessions, so we need skill in brief interventions. We are one of many services that the GP could call on, which can influence what kind of referrals are made. If we are regarded as a valued part of the practice team, the collaboration can work extremely well, with shared understanding and mutual respect. Such a situation may, however, will be hard-won and it will require work to protect and maintain it.

GPs are extremely busy and can be very difficult to get hold of, and often meetings, even if all agree in principle that they are useful, are not held as regularly as would be helpful. Counselling can be a place where cases are sent when felt to be troublesome and unrewarding because not amenable to the usual array of medical interventions. This can offer relief to GPs who cannot give their patients the time needed to explore issues more deeply, but can then become an institutional positioning of the counselling that invites problematic dynamics. We can be the recipient of projections from the medical staff dictated by a sense of failure, and/or of disappointment with and contempt for the unresponsive patients. There can then be an unconscious desire for the counselling to fail, even if accompanied by a strong conscious desire for it to work.

By their nature and training, most medical staff will be familiar with and at home with a medical model, in which symptoms are treated and illnesses cured. In contrast the more psychological view would hold that some physical symptoms and disturbances may be the expression of strains in the mental, emotional and relationship lives of the patients, which require understanding rather than direct treatment. There will naturally be medical staff in tune with this latter view, and we can assume that any practice that has employed a counsellor will have already made a commitment to the value of a psychological approach. We as practice counsellors can do a great deal to enhance psychodynamic thinking in the work of the practice as a whole. However, we need to be able to make good connections with the way the other professionals think, and to learn how to use the language of the other staff so that understandings can be more fully shared. Respect for the professionalism and expertise of the doctors and nurses even, or rather especially, if they might have different views about a case, will be crucial.

Laura (15) was taken to her GP by her mother, after a period in which Laura had not been sleeping at all well. The GP had referred her for counselling as he felt that it would be more helpful to explore the reasons behind the difficulty than to prescribe any medication, which is what the family had imagined they would get. The nurse also saw Laura to advise on relaxation techniques and bedtime routines. In the counselling it was uncovered how Laura was anxious and angry following her brother having left for university, which left her feeling responsible for her mother, with increased ambivalence about her own eventual leaving home. She had not been conscious of the nature of the anxieties preventing her from falling asleep, only that she just couldn't get properly relaxed and let herself go. Once some of the underlying concerns were put into words and made more accessible, she was able to rest more easily.

In a contrasting situation, the counsellor in the GP practice was able to offer some brief work with a number of children who had all been witnesses to a car accident in which a child had been killed. These were not children who required the specialist services of a mental health clinic, but they needed some help to process their feelings about such a traumatic incident. The practice counsellor was well placed to help, without the children feeling labeled – the offer coming from the GP practice enabled them to access support within the familiar and local service that normalized the provision, both for them and for their parents.

As yet there are not many surgeries that employ specifically trained child and adolescent practitioners, so it may be that an adult-trained counsellor needs to adapt her work for the younger age group. This may mean that further training or at least specialist supervision is indicated. Some symptoms such as depression and self-harm manifest themselves in most age groups, so there will be a great deal of common ground and certain aspects of the same thinking can be used. However, an adolescent's depression is likely to need a different approach from that of an isolated 50-year-old man or an elderly widow. A child's psychosomatic pain is likely to require a different sort of intervention than a 40 year old's. As is evident from the subject matter of this book, there is a great deal about working with children and adolescents that is very different from working with adults (Kegerreis 2006). A counsellor in a GP practice who is trained in adult work may have to seek out specialist training and/or supervision to be able to fulfill the role effectively.

## Other medical settings – hospitals, hospices, etc.

In other medical settings the role of the counsellor is more likely to be as an aid to the child or adolescent coping with and adapting to a medical condition or disability, or maybe to work with bereavement. Here there will be much less of an expectation of cure or a medical view of the counselling itself, but still the work will be experienced as an adjunct to the physical interventions. The counselling will be carrying many of the feelings derived from the medical interventions, and we need to be able to tune into the impact of these on the child, over and above the nature of the problem bringing him to the work. If the medical treatment has been experienced as intrusive and persecutory it is very likely that these dynamics will be brought into the counselling relationship, and the work can help a great deal if these dynamics can be understood and worked with rather than avoided.

Medical interventions always require cooperation and compliance from the patients, and this is even more a feature if there is a chronic condition that will need prolonged and often uncomfortable commitment. As a counsellor we can help promote this compliance. To do so we must fully connect with the fear, rage, helplessness and disappointment of the child or adolescent who is faced with such a painful situation. For example, Christos (18) had thalassaemia, a blood disorder that requires repeated transfusions. He sometimes struggled to comply with his treatment, even though he knew that failure to do so could have fatal results. Counselling helped him come to terms with his feelings about the disease and its impact on their lives. This included his rage with his parents for handing down to him such faulty bodily equipment, mourning the carefree adolescence that in fantasy he would have had without it, his terror about his future, his fury at being so dependent when he was trying to establish adulthood, his painful awareness of vulnerability when developmentally he would otherwise be in the grip of normal adolescent omnipotence and assumed immortality.

Such work can literally save lives, as being able to process these feelings can help young people like Christos stay in compliance with their treatment.

One of the skills in working with such children is to balance our awareness of the impact of the illness or disability with the perception of the other ingredients of the child's difficulties. We can easily fall into the trap of only seeing the disability and not the child, or alternatively maybe to flip to the other extreme and only see the child and lose track of the physical damage (Hoxter 1986). This is always a problem when a child comes with a particular label. It applies strongly to disabled or ill children, but such a concern also arises with sexually-abused children (Dyke 1987). One contribution of counselling to the child's overall welfare can often be that he feels as if there he is seen as a whole, rather than just as a walking example of a condition. However, equally it can be the one place where the full emotional impact of the condition can be considered. For example, if a child is in recovery and all the adults around them are so relieved that he is going to survive, the counselling might be the only place the child feels it is understood how much he has lost, and how mixed and confused his feelings might be about his future. If parents and doctors are both feeling that the best result they could hope for has occurred, it can be very hard for them to hear or otherwise perceive that the child is still reeling from the trauma and may have grave difficulties in resuming his developmental path.

In addition, the traumatic impact of a child's illness on his parents can be such that he may feel that he has to manage his own traumatized feelings without further burdening them. Their grief and anger can make it difficult for them to be able to process their child's complex responses. Counselling can offer so much in such a scenario, providing the child with a much-needed outlet for problematic feelings, and hopefully paving the way to better communication between child and parent.

# Other possible settings

There is scope for child and adolescent counsellors to be usefully employed in a range of other settings. For example, marital and relationship counselling agencies (such as Relate, 1–1) are very aware of the impact of relationship breakup on the children, but there is as yet little in the way of child or adolescent counselling on offer in most regions. A counsellor trained to work with children could be a welcome addition to couples counselling and mediation services offered to families in crisis. Children, during the process of family breakup, can often feel unheard and ignored, as their parents are so overwhelmed and preoccupied by their own difficulties. The children themselves are often deeply upset, confused, frightened and guilty, and can be torn by loyalty conflicts. Offering sensitive listening and facilitation can be of great value in preventing later disturbance.

Hospices and bereavement services do often provide a counselling service, and some offer specialist help for children (e.g. Zig-Zag and Winston's Wish) but there is scope for very much more to be made available. Some issues will, of course, be shared by all who have lost a loved one, but there is a need for specialist skills in working with bereaved young people (Blundell in Baruch 2001). The level of the child's understanding of death can be so varied and the nature of the loss of a parent or sibling for a child so different from that for adults. We need to do full justice to the impact of the loss, which in the case of a parent is so massive in its range of both practical and emotional meanings. The loss of a sibling is likely also to be fraught with fears for oneself, changes in the relationship with parents and difficult issues of rivalry. Yet we also need to keep in mind the developmental thrust to move onward and to get on with life. In some ways this is not so different from the same conflict in adults, but specialists in child and adolescent work will be better placed to pick up on the particular internal and external issues for children in bereavement.

Wherever we work with children and adolescents, our psychodynamic thinking will be the bedrock of our practice. However, as this chapter has shown, each setting will bring with it particular flavours and particular organizational dynamics, which necessarily will have an impact on the nature of the counselling offered, and on the roles available for us to take up both with the professionals around us and the young people.

# 14

# Short-Term and Time-Limited Work

One of the differences usually identified between counselling and psychotherapy relates to the issue of length of treatment. In general, psychotherapy is more likely to be long-term and/or open-ended. Counselling is often short-term and/or time-limited. It is useful to be clear that there are two different elements at play here, the actual length of time and the question as to whether there is a set time frame before the work starts. Open-ended work can be short-term, and long-term work can be time-limited, as in a contract for 2 years of psychotherapy. There can of course also be short-term time-limited work, for example if what is offered is 6 sessions of counselling. Different problems and opportunities arise with each kind.

There are differences in the approach to issues of time between the trainings for psychotherapy and counselling. This has an effect on the mind-set of psychotherapists and counsellors, particularly at the start of their careers. In psychoanalytic psychotherapy trainings there is a requirement to see a certain number of patients for a certain time. Trainees typically have to see patients regularly for the 18 months or 2 years before being eligible for qualification. Even a small shortfall can mean that that work may not count towards the clinical requirement and keeping the therapy going can feel like an end in itself. In contrast, while counselling trainings may specify some minimum time with a client, many do not. Overall clinical hours are the more usual measure, with numbers of hours counting towards accreditation with the British Association of Counselling and Psychotherapy rather than any predicated length of treatment for any particular client.

These differences in training have their effect on the attitude towards the length of engagement. Not surprisingly the emphasis on long-term training patients, together with the predominant underlying thinking and literature belonging to the tradition of lengthy analyses, gives rise to a tendency amongst psychotherapists, especially newly-trained ones, to start a new treatment with an outlook implicitly (or explicitly) geared to engaging the patient in long-term work, helping them see the need for it, 'catching their interest' in starting the long haul. This undoubtedly has great value, in that it enables work of great depth and subtlety to be done. However, there can also be a tendency for longevity in treatment in itself being seen as some kind of indicator of success, as it implies a serious piece of work has been undertaken and engagement in this successfully established. It can be overlooked or there can be scepticism that important change can be achieved in relatively shorter timescales.

Counsellors, on the other hand, can sometimes be led unhelpfully into a mind-set where retaining patients for an extended period is not expected and therefore the possible need for it is not given sufficient emphasis. There can be a tendency not to pay enough attention to the subtleties of the developing transference and countertransference with the potential for working through the difficulties and gaining insight into the re-enactments that long-term work can provide. The value of long-term work, with its offer of a truly deep reworking of inner conflicts, can be underestimated.

Nonetheless, if working in a hard-pressed agency, which is struggling with waiting lists and resource shortages, leading to a need for 'throughput', the ability to work short-term is often required, and the capacity to adapt psychoanalytic thinking to short-term and time-limited work is invaluable.

The value of being able to work short-term applies to work with any age group, but is potentially even more relevant if working with children and adolescents rather than adults. As has been outlined, with the younger client group, we are still dealing with a fluid system rather than a set of defences and an internal organization that has been embedded for maybe decades. We do not yet have to deal with the additional burdens of years of pain, regret and accumulated loss and damage that adults have to contend with once they start to change (Kegerreis 2006). Sometimes the problems are just arising, with families in flux or traumatic events just happening, or sometimes, as already mentioned, our task is to free up the obstacles to ordinary maturation that is temporarily stalled or blocked. We have the developmental force on our side, and the natural hopefulness of still being young with relatively little to regret and mourn can help the young people re-engage with what is healthy in themselves and in their outside world.

It is a commonplace that timescales are experienced by children as much longer than by adults. To them a month, a term or a year is felt to be a far more substantial amount of time than it appears to us as adults. However, despite this there is in fact less opportunity for 'timelessness' in childhood than later in life. An adult can drift through the years without fully taking on board how much of their life is passing, until perhaps something like a bereavement or their biological clock reminds them that they do not have forever to sort things out. However, a child has school terms and school years relentlessly reminding them of how they are moving on. In working with children, even if we are not working with explicit restrictions on session numbers, we can never avoid the need to think about time being in short supply. Children need to make use of their education, they need to be ready for secondary transfer, for public exams or for leaving school or the care system. So even if time is not explicitly rationed, we always need to have in mind that the work is urgent, and that it is necessary to help as much as possible in as short a time as possible.

Even if the work is open-ended, giving any impression of time-lessness in the work can be counterproductive. With older children and adolescents it is often a vital element of the work to make sure that time is brought in as a 'character', as some of the problems that bring them to counselling relate explicitly to their responses to time passing and their growing up. As described earlier, many difficulties that can appear as academic or behavioural symptoms can be disguised protests against having to relinquish being a child, or a desperate expression of anxiety about not feeling equipped for the next stage of growing up. An understanding of this element can be the key to helping the young person face their fears and grievances in a way that can free them to move forward more confidently. The counselling needs to be tuning into the relationship with time expressed by the child both explicitly and through the presenting symptom.

## Agencies and time

Schools and some services offering counselling in schools often work with the assumption that the work will fit into the school year, but in other agencies the work is open-ended. Some schools (mostly using non-psychodynamic approaches) have 6- or 12-week contracts as a norm. Child and Family Consultation Centres and adolescent support services sometimes do and sometimes do not specify a time frame. Some adolescent services, such as the Young People's Consultation Service at the Tavistock Clinic for example, operate a 4-session service, which explicitly uses a therapeutic consultation model. Here consultation is offered as the therapeutic encounter, rather than a counselling contract.

Thinking about a suitable time frame needs to take into account the kind of work children can manage. Small children who use play need time to establish a relationship, as they cannot simply explain or talk through the reasons for their being in counselling. There can be a more explicit and organizationally sanctioned idea that young children need a nurturing depth of emotional connection and support, rather than a more focused problem-solving approach. Generally speaking, the younger the child the more likely it is that significant improvement will require a longer period of work.

## Time-limited work

Even in open-ended psychodynamic work the clock is still metaphorically a presence in the room. Each session will have a beginning, a middle and an end accordingly. Children and adolescents, like adults, develop a keen sense of time. In each session they will relate to the counsellor in a way that is arranged around the beginning, in which the focus (often unconsciously) is on the gap and absence since the last session, the middle where the developmental work of this particular session itself can have a place, and the end, when the separation is being led up to. There will be holidays and other breaks that bring time in and make it a feature in the work. However, in time-limited work, the presence of the **end** of the work is always present, as well as the passage of the sessions and the terms. There is an explicit knowledge that the relationship will end in a certain amount of time, and in this way the time frame becomes a most important element in the work (Coren 1996; Mander 2000). There will be a more marked transference to time itself at work, with the child's or adolescent's relationship with time and their own experience of time passing having its own powerful role to play.

From the beginning of the encounter, the issue of the outcome of the work will also be more strongly present. This is the case with open-ended work too, but with the ending not specified from the outset this does not have the same impact. The very fact of the time limit will imply at one and the same time a hopefulness that things can be sorted out in a specified time, but also a sense of potential failure that will have an additional concreteness to it. The child or even more keenly the adolescent will already have an idea of how this relationship is going to end up, coloured by their past experiences and felt impact of the course of other relationships. Adolescents particularly may have a defensive need to prove adults impotent, and the time limit may exacerbate this, making it too difficult for any vulnerability-inducing hope to develop.

On the other hand, for developmental reasons adolescents may be wary of letting another adult become important to them and to develop new dependencies. They therefore may be more confident about entering time-limited work when open-ended work would possibly be too anxiety provoking or felt to be 'trapping them back in' when they are trying to 'move out'.

In any kind of counselling it is often useful to ask at some point, or to consider out loud, what the client may imagine the outcome to be. This will often reveal an aspect of the relationship that might not otherwise have become obvious for a long time and in time-limited work this can be even more useful as there isn't the time to let this emerge (Mak-Pearce in Baruch 2001). It may be that the child is inwardly convinced that the counsellor, like others, will get fed up with him, will find someone more interesting to see, will give up in despair, will get furious and kick him out, etc. Alternatively there could be an unspoken hope of idealized rescue, of all problems being solved and intercessions made, a champion against teachers or parents, someone who will so completely see the client's point of view that they will not have to challenge themselves at all. In short-term time-limited work, these issues of anticipated outcome will have a particularly keenly-felt quality as the outcome is only just out of view.

What is key in any time-limited work, whether of 6 weeks or a year's duration, is that we keep the time frame clearly in mind. This is sometimes more difficult than it may seem. There can be such a wish to be able to provide what the client needs that the limits are 'forgotten' or avoided. We may ourselves have angry feelings about having to limit the work and then conscious or unconscious mechanisms lead to the time frame getting ignored until too late. This can lead to the negative feelings about the shortage of time being transferred onto the outside pressures, whether this is the agency itself or the funding authorities, etc., rather than being more fruitfully taken up in the work. It can be difficult at times to tell whether a feeling in us that there is not enough time is a valid response to major and long-established difficulties, or are countertransference enactments of projected despair. It is certainly true that a short amount of work may not make much headway with such problems, and in some cases long-term work is urgently needed. However, it may equally be that the feelings of hopelessness need to be thought about carefully and not allowed to sabotage what can be achieved. It is often surprising how much can be done with only a few sessions. If client and counsellor both know they only have a few sessions, it concentrates the mind enormously, and enables a style of work that is more active and focused and can be of great value.

One area in which short-term time-limited work has to differ is in its use of the transference. In longer-term work we might hear about difficulties with other people, and think with the client about how this might be referring at least in part to how they are feeling about us, and gradually pull more and more of the experience of the child into the room where it can be most immediately looked at (see Meltzer 1967 on the *Gathering of the Transference*). For example, Claire (12) came in after a half-term break and talked about a teacher ignoring her when she was in trouble with her dreaded maths and this teacher having a favourite pupil on whom she spent too much attention. In psychotherapy and longer-term counselling this might usefully be looked at by thinking with her about her experience of my having been away the week before (in fantasy with a favoured child) when we both knew that the half-term break was going to be particularly difficult. This is a straightforward example of how we might use transference thinking, so as to help the child manage difficult feelings as they have arisen in the here and now, where we can work on them together.

There is no time for the transference to be developed like this within short-term work. We do not have the luxury of being able to foster slowly the unique emotional connections and enactments that show the child's inner world at work. What we do have to work with is the transference that is immediately available, both in our experience of the relationship created in the room as well as the configurations that emerge from the information given to us about outside relationships by the child. If we only have a few sessions, we can most usefully engage the child by working from the inside out, rather than the other way around. By this I mean we might work more directly from the experience of being with the child, and then extrapolate out to how this might inform both of us about how he relates to others. This then could interest him and draw attention to his relationships and make him think about their own perceptions and interpretations. The perception of his immediate style of relating and our own experience in the countertransference can bring forcefully to the child's attention how he functions with others. This can open up useful thinking that has a real bite to it because it is alive between us, as well as relevant to outside difficulties.

Nadil (14) comes in and immediately bombards the counsellor with a breathless account of drama and emergency (personal but not seriously worrying), seemingly oblivious to the fact that the counsellor is new to him and he does not know if she is trustworthy or not. The counsellor might at some point alert him to this and wonder if this happens elsewhere and is how he perhaps manages in other relationships. It could be an indication of a range of important relationship issues. It may be that he is demonstrating that he is so absorbed in his own internal world that he is insufficiently attentive to the people to whom he is relating. It could be that he is working with an internal longing for an instant merger/match that does away with interpersonal distance at a stroke, and cannot deal with the 'gap' between himself and – at its root – his mother. Or it could be that he idealizes people at first in order to protect them and himself from a critical and destructive part of himself, or in order to set up an inevitable final betrayal. Or that he needs to grab attention with drama and immediacy to deal with fears of rejection or being insufficiently interesting or important to bother with. Whatever the underlying set of feelings emerging as being behind his presentation in the room, the exploration of it as a shared experience can be a route into accurately focused work. If we alert the child as to what is being brought into his relationship with us, and wonder about it as an indication of what may be affecting his other relationships, we then have a focus that has been established together and that will hopefully have engaged his interest.

Time-limited work needs a focus, whether this is explicitly the problem as brought through the referral or, more usefully, the problem as reformulated in the process of assessment (Malan 1979; Mander 2000; Coren 2001). This means that the work done needs to be related to the formulated problem, even if at first it does not seem so closely connected. The psychodynamic model of the mind and relationships implies that issues are always going to be interconnected in some way, so a deep belief in this can help us find a focus without unduly lamenting all that is left out. It is almost always possible to bring the problems discussed into relationship with the central theme without undue distortion.

What it does mean, however, is that there may be major areas of a child's or adolescent's life that one accepts will not be explicitly addressed, and that work that could usefully be done may not be undertaken for the time being.

For example, Rosie (15) came for counselling because of extreme pre-exam stress. Because it was already half way through the final term she was offered a 6-week contract. She was a bright girl who had done well and had good predicted grades. In discussion it turned out that her father had left home when she was 12 and she had felt intensely rejected at first but had since got on fine, in fact had felt that life was much better than it would have been if he had stayed at home, as he would have been much stricter with her about her social life. What upset her most about her difficulty in working was that 'she would be letting him down' if she did poorly in the GCSEs. It became clear that Rosie associated exam success with pleasing father, who had been successful himself at university and who looked to her to continue in his footsteps. It was not hard to see that her sudden block in work was caused by the re-emergence of her buried hurt and anger at just the crucial moment, resurfacing as the exams came into focus and threatening the outcome she most feared of letting him down (as she had felt let down by him).

It was clear as she talked that her relationships with her mother, boyfriends and school friends were all somewhat affected by difficulties which had early roots. She had grown up denying hurt, anger and vulnerability and had developed an image for herself and others as tough, capable and amiable, which while partly true, was at considerable cost as it meant suppressing much that was less acceptable. Had this been long-term work there would have been scope for exploring these issues at depth and working them through in the transference. However, it was also quite possible to relate this, without distorting the key issues, to the central focus. This was on the integrating of Rosie's vulnerable, angry and hurt feelings more comfortably and consciously into her image of herself. By becoming aware of her anger with father the path was cleared to allowing herself to begin to forgive him for leaving which, despite her conscious acceptance, she had never done. She also could begin to forgive herself enough for having been so vulnerable to be hurt by him. The focus on her feelings around her father and how this related to her sense of herself was broad enough to enable sufficient work to be done to stop these feelings sabotaging herself and to free her up to do well in her exams. More could have been done in longer-term work, but the 6-week time frame was helpful in keeping a core focus in view, and in this case was sufficient to the task.

# Open-ended short-term work

In many settings there may be the freedom to see children for as long or short a time as is felt by both counsellor and client to be useful. This is therefore not time-limited work, but it may well turn out to be short-term. The first session with a new referral may be the only session or the first of a relationship lasting many months or even years, if the setting allows for this. This gives the initial phases of the work a great freedom, as it is always possible that what is being conducted is a therapeutic consultation (Winnicott 1971), which will be all the child needs. It also gives rise to a particular kind of technique at the beginning, which is more of an assess-ment/consultation technique using psychodynamic thinking, rather than the less active, more reflective style more suitable for an explicitly long-term referral (Chapter 15).

In such a consultation the question of what has brought the child to us is the first obvious focus. Usually this brings out the present-ing problem, which may be a current or school-based concern. What is most helpful is for us to explore this as best we can, clarify-ing and getting the basic shape of the issues into a more visible form. It is often helpful then to suggest that there is a step back so that a family tree can be made (Chapter 4). Nearly always this gives us information that directly connects with the presenting problem, either by showing a clear answer to the 'why now' question (see Chapter 15) or by there being obvious parallels between the quali-ties and shapes of the relationships/problems presented as current, and the qualities and shapes of key elements in the child's relation-ship/history with her family.

For example, in Harry's case (12), he was becoming distressed in school because he was preoccupied and worried about an older uncle, who was an alcoholic. In the initial meeting with me, he looked down almost all the time, speaking in a flat tone without much emotion, although showing some animation when talking of the 'bad guys' in his family tree but still seeming extremely burdened. What emerged from the family tree was a complex and eventful history, particularly concerning the central role in his mind of this uncle, who had lost links with his son and, although now not drinking was a constant source of anxiety and concern for Harry. I was intrigued but puzzled as to why this uncle loomed so large in his mind. It came over strongly that it was essential to Harry that the family should stand by the uncle and not write him off, as his mother and aunt were close to doing. He also spoke of his grandmother, whom he feared had felt neglected when she was ill. A great fear emerged regarding both his uncle and grandmother that they might think they were not loved. This had to be avoided at all costs. Harry seemed to be an overly conscientious and caring boy who had taken on the role of the loving support to anyone vulnerable in the family. He seemed burdened but saintly.

At the end of the first session he had spoken a great deal, but still seemed weighed down, and I did not feel I had understood the underlying dynamics sufficiently. However, when Harry returned a week later, his manner was quite different. He held his head much higher, met my gaze much more often, and broke out from time to time into a wickedly mischievous smile. This proved to be most valuable, as suddenly I could see sides of him that had been buried in the first session, and this was the key to the understanding that had been elusive the first time.

It emerged that he saw his uncle as the most troublesome in his mother's family. Harry thought that he was the most troublesome in his family too. Having had the saintly suffering Harry in the room a week ago had made this seem most unlikely! Suddenly it was clear that his anxiety about this uncle was, although quite genuine, most importantly an expression of Harry's fear that he was too much for his mother and that he was at risk of being cut off from love and support, like his uncle and the sick grandmother. He told me stories of the bad things he had done, and we were able to think together about his anxieties about growing up with all the dangers and opportunities it presented. He spoke of his fear that he would turn out like his uncle, unable to cope or to manage his own impulses.

In the first session he had said that it was impossible to talk to his mother about his feelings as he feared she would be too upset and cut the uncle off completely. However, by the third session, he had managed to talk to her and this had helped. He then spoke about friendship wrangles at school and talked vividly about a friend who was getting into trouble and in a bit of a mess. While this could have been taken up as an invitation to start on a new agenda of helping him with his friendships, and/or that the boy in a mess was a projected version of Harry himself, I did neither. I took the talk about school friendships as being exactly what a boy his age should be preoccupied with, and a sign that normal development had been resumed. I saw the talk about the friend, as is often the case, as being a sign that he could think of others who needed help now.

We agreed to finish the counselling. He had changed a great deal in three weeks. The uncle had been put back in his place, communication with Harry's parents had been resumed, and teenage life had reclaimed him. It appeared that the work was done.

In another case, Ayesha (15) was referred to the counsellor as she was becoming tearful and avoidant in lessons, often having to leave the class. It was known that she had been involved in some kind of assaultive incident over a year before, but there was no obvious reason why she was in such distress now.

After an inhibited start she managed to tell me about the incident, in which she had been sexually molested by boys whom she knew were 'rough' but had thought she could handle. She had been initially angry about it all, but not upset. She did not know why she was upset about it again now. For a long time she had not been, so no-one, including her, understood why it was bad again now. As the discussion continued, I thought with her about how she had not let herself know at the time how serious the incident had been. The trauma of being assaulted and helpless had been bad, but what was additionally awful for her was that what she had lost was a whole image of herself as being able to 'handle' things that other girls were too timid to take on.

I put to her that what had been stolen from her that day was not only a cherished fantasy about herself, but even more importantly a whole set of defences against feeling afraid or vulnerable. Up until then she had been able to pretend to herself and others that she could handle anything, and even afterwards had made out that she could manage even this frightening incident. Now whenever she felt stressed she found herself thinking back to the incident with rage, not least at herself for being upset. She could no longer so effectively deploy these defences in the face of current worries. This was the extra ingredient for which she could not forgive the boys – the fact that they had taken away her way of protecting herself against these vulnerable feelings.

She left this session much lighter of step. She was quite chastened by what I had said to her, which was painful to hear. She said, 'There is so much more to think about, but I have to think about it, I see that.'

This is an example of something that can frequently occur. A young person comes to the counsellor as a result of some traumatic incident. The trauma itself naturally needs to be given proper weight, but what they are often affected by is not simply the incident itself, but the way this has interfered with a cherished self-image. They have often discovered a potential to hate and to feel violent towards someone that now has to be assimilated into their new idea of who they are. They have also felt helpless in a way that crashes through the (perhaps necessary) omnipotence of adolescence, and this has shaken their ability to muster useful defences over lesser issues.

In such cases, it is often enough to work together to reveal these underlying issues and the young people can go away and do the rest themselves. It gives them a new way of understanding the inchoate distress they are feeling, makes it think-about-able, and in many cases this is all the help they need.

There are obvious elements in this kind of work that are closely connected with what is described in the following chapter on assessment. A therapeutic consultation in whatever setting in which the problem is identified, the background explored, connections made and the emotional and developmental issues clarified can be powerfully therapeutic in itself. It can be sufficient to launch the child or adolescent into doing the rest of the work within his or her own circle without further counselling.

However, it is not useful to assume that all problems can be dealt with in short-term work. In some children the nature of the difficulty is much deeper and a more substantial piece of work is needed. Alongside helping children quickly, if at all possible, it is just as important to help the child settle into longer-term work if that is what is called for. With younger children who need help in developing a more secure sense of self, addressing quite primitive confusions and terrors, or in managing early damage enough to engage helpfully with any adult, there is not going to be a great deal that can be done in a short time. With older adolescents the damage may be deep and long-established, and for a major reorganization of their inner worlds much longer-term work may be required. Using the psychodynamic framework we should be equipped to do both, as and when indicated.

# 15

# ASSESSMENT

It may seem odd to have left the topic of assessment until near the end of this book. This is partly because those at the beginning of their career as counsellors, for whom this book is predominantly aimed, are likely to be working in agencies where the assessment thinking is going to be done by a more experienced practitioner. It is also because assessment requires much of the understanding that is outlined in the earlier chapters. So although assessment has to take place at the beginning of the encounter with the child, this chapter would not be well placed at the beginning of the book.

Relating to this, it is during the assessment process that skilled supervision has the utmost importance. Supervision is key to setting up the best possible start to the work, both in order to tune in more accurately as to what is going on in the child, and to assess the appropriateness of the provision.

When a child first walks into the counselling room, we have a complex task to perform. Even if the meeting is not in any formal sense labelled as an assessment, in that counselling is understood to be on offer, there needs to be what could be termed 'assessment thinking' going on, encompassing a range of different questions which I have used to provide the structure for this chapter. Hinshelwood 1991, Holmes 1995 and Waddell 2002 are useful for a more detailed consideration of psychodynamic assessments.

## What is the problem?

We might already know something about the nature of the problem prompting the child's arrival from a letter or referral form, but even so we need to find out from the child himself how he perceives the problem that has brought him here. We cannot assume we know what the problem is, even if there is ostensibly a clear reason for the referral. We cannot engage a child on the basis of what the referrer has described as the problem as the child's own idea of why they are there might be very different (Chapter 10).

Moreover, even if the stated reason for the referral is something the child might agree with, such as a recent bereavement, this does not tell us anything about what the bereavement means to the child, precisely how the bereavement is affecting him or what feelings about the bereavement are causing the difficulties. Bereavement in itself is not a reason for counselling, although it might well be a cause of a difficulty that is. Feelings of sadness and loss may be painful, but they might not be nearly as difficult to bear as anger or guilty relief. The pressing concern may not be the bereavement as such, but the way in which this has uncovered previously concealed difficulties about a divorce or a neglectful parent. A child may be suffering from not being able to make sense of what has happened, or by the way in which the bereavement has crashed into previous certainties and left them painfully anxious or in strenuous denial. The bereavement is not the problem – the impact of it might be but will be different in every case.

Notwithstanding the importance of finding out and defining with the child himself what the problem is, it is also part of the assessment process to make the best possible use of the sources of information that are available. One might want, or indeed need, to make a multi-faceted assessment, using not just the encounter with the child, but reports from teachers, GPs or other professionals. It is also nearly always useful, and often essential, to meet the family or the child with the parents. This is partly so we can gain a much fuller understanding of the background to the child's problems and their impact on those around them. The meeting with the child and the engagement process is then set in the context of a larger understanding of the child's world. This then needs to be woven together with the more personal elements learned about in the first session(s) to make an informed judgement on what the problem is, as well as the other questions outlined in this chapter.

As has already been seen in the passage on engagement and consent, the task of defining and framing the problem is in itself a most powerful part of the therapeutic process. It has been said of consultation to organizations that 'once the problem is defined the consultation is complete' (Wilson 1991) and although this is not in any simple sense applicable to counselling, there is a sense in which once the problem is defined the work has already seriously started.

# Whose problem is it?

The question as to whose problem it is can be a tricky one. We need to work out in meeting a child or adolescent whether he himself needs help or whether his being sent for counselling is a substitute for some other important action. The most obvious possibility is that the problem is not in any simple sense the child's but one belonging to the whole family. This could mostly call for clarifying the role of the counselling, but in some cases it could be that another intervention would be preferable.

For example, Patricia (13) came to counselling troubled by the increasingly fierce rows between her parents. Patricia appeared to be reacting in a straightforward way to difficult circumstances and was not apparently herself a disturbed child. This did not imply that help would not be offered, but it might mean that we would think about how to try to engage the family with local family support services or couples counselling. The work with Patricia might then be more geared to helping her process her own sense of the family situation and its meaning to her. We would be trying to limit its impact on her and her own development, rather than working on internal conflicts that were preventing her moving on. This may appear an overly simplistic divide as there will most usually be elements of the two at work, but it is still helpful to keep these different tasks distinct in our thinking.

On the other hand we might be presented with a child who is struggling with a family situation which makes counselling contra-indicated. This could be where the level of violence or neglect is such that there need to be other interventions and the child coming to counselling is being used as a way of ignoring and avoiding a larger and more important issue. If a parent is seriously not coping as a carer, for example because of alcohol or drug abuse, it could be that offering a child counselling, however well-intentioned, becomes part of a general avoidance of tackling the central issue.

Children in such difficult family circumstances might need all the defences they have to cope. As already made clear, defences have a purpose, and it is only helpful for a child to become less defended if these defences have become stuck and outdated and are therefore now doing more harm than good. If we ask a child to face more clearly a situation that should be addressed and ameliorated, we could be colluding with an idea in the network that something is being done, when we are potentially putting the child in a worse situation. We are asking too much of children if we expect them to work on issues that the adults around them shrink from facing. In the worst versions of this scenario, parents and professionals can use the possibility of counselling as an attempt to escape from an impasse. The offer of counselling can become a collusion with an avoidance of something more powerfully needed and can actually help everyone avoid a more potentially anxiety provoking or threatening course of action. Sadly the pressure on funds can also lead to referral to counselling being used by the network as a cheaper alternative to more expensive options.

For example, social services referred two girls aged 5 and 7 for counselling at a community family service. It became clear to the counsellor in the course of two sessions, that the girls were showing signs of being seriously deprived, and of suffering from inconsistency and neglect from their mother. In discussion with the social worker, it emerged that Social Services were aware that the mother needed major amounts of help in managing family life in a more containing manner, and knew that the girls were left alone for inappropriate amounts of time and were given little attention. The counsellor felt that to take them on for emotional work of their own would be colluding in Social Services not providing the intensive resources needed to support this family, and so put her energies into helping them make a case for more input to the mother and to the family as a whole.

In another case (Kegerreis 1987), two small children in foster care were referred for psychotherapeutic assessment after one had been abused and both had been exposed to a sexually abusive environment in their family. What emerged from the assessment is that it was felt to be too soon to offer direct work with the children. It was felt that they needed to settle into the experience of being in a family with good boundaries and effective parenting, and to see if they were able to make good use of this, rather than rushing to offer them work of their own away from the family. Psychotherapy might well emerge as being needed in time, but it seemed better for them first to build good links with good carers in their external world. Later one would be able to ascertain if the internal damage was too great for this good care to address. Support for the foster carers to help them manage the disturbing impact of these girls' behaviour and history emerged as a better use of resources.

There will be other cases when it becomes clear through individual or family meetings that it would be more helpful to work with the whole family instead of with the child individually. As has already been made clear, family dynamics are frequently a major underlying reason for the onset of the child's difficulties and they are also likely to be a factor in maintaining the presenting problem, whatever its origins. Families may be consciously very unhappy with a child's behaviour or worried by their distress, while still unconsciously playing a powerful part in keeping that child exactly as they are. A child may be acting out a distress that is primarily located between the parents, or playing a part that, despite creating its own problems, acts to hold the family together or to allow the family to avoid something terribly painful. Part of any assessment needs to be whether individual work with the child will have any chance of working, if family dynamics are not addressed, as there may be forces at work which make it essential for the family for the child to carry on with his role. It is beyond the scope of this book to explore the psychodynamic work that can be done with families, but using the same core ideas and techniques outlined here, if the whole family can be engaged a counsellor can do powerful work to release the families' resources and free the child to develop more healthily.

If working in a school, we need also to wonder if what brings the child to us is more the school's problem rather than the child's. We may be receiving the same kind of referrals from the same sources, for example of disruptive children from one particular teacher or section of the school, or there might be a series of referrals around incidents of bullying. In these scenarios it might be worth thinking about whether the school is using the counselling to address, or perhaps more accurately to avoid addressing, a problem with classroom management, a stage of development (e.g. transition from primary school) or a systemic aspect of the school's culture that is not being thought about adequately (Chapter 12). This does not necessarily mean that we would decide not to see the child, but it might indicate that it would be worthwhile to consider some other intervention that could promote more productive thinking about these wider issues.

## Is counselling the right resource?

Once the problem is clarified and it is established satisfactorily that it is in some significant way the child's problem, or at least that helping the child directly is a good option, the next question is whether counselling is what is called for. This is another multifaceted issue. It includes the issues mentioned above relating to whose problem it is, as the answer to this question would be an indication as to whether family, social work or education-based input would be preferable. However, there is more to consider. First and foremost we need to assess the level of risk the young person is in. Obviously if the child is being hurt or sexually abused it is clear that we need urgently to notify the right people in accordance with Safeguarding procedures.

We need also to ascertain whether there is a risk of suicide or breakdown. The issues around risk assessment are too complex to go into here, but part of the initial exploration has to be whether what we as counsellors can offer will be sufficient to hold the child and to address the seriousness of what is troubling them. If there are clear suicidal or self-harm issues, including serious eating disorders, that need medical intervention then we must make sure this is accessed. To offer counselling on its own would be irresponsible and a dereliction of professional care.

If suicide or serious self-harm are not immediately seen as risk factors, there are still a series of questions that need to be considered. Is the degree of difficulty such that a counsellor in this setting can offer enough, or is more intensive psychotherapy indicated? Is this child or adolescent showing signs of being or becoming psychotic? In other words, is the child's degree of contact with reality sufficient for counselling to be appropriate, or is there something more seriously awry that needs a psychiatric assessment? We need to be alert as to whether there are indications that the work of counselling could precipitate a breakdown, so that, even if the client could use the counselling, once a week work might stir up a great deal but would not be able to provide adequate holding once defences start to be lowered. We need an idea of whether there is sufficient support in this young person's network and system to allow them to become vulnerable in the way that counselling can require and also whether the network can cope with change. There needs to be enough of a structure and sufficient ongoing connection with the real world to make it safe for them to embark on internal exploration. It takes skill and careful judgement to assess the underlying vulnerability of a young person who is highly defended, but this is just as important as it is with one who is openly depressed or self-destructive.

There might be other practical reasons why counselling is not the right resource. For example, if a child comes to a school counsellor when already seriously school-avoidant or phobic, with attendance problems such that they are rarely in school for the counselling, then it is likely that the work will not be viable. Educational Welfare, Home-school Liaison or Social Services might need to be accessed to put in considerable work before counselling could have much of a chance. This is not to say that attendance issues are beyond a school counsellor. This is clearly not the case and the opportunity for their fears and hostilities in school to be addressed in counselling is often a vital part of bringing a child back into regular attendance. However, it needs to be faced that we can not magically turn a child's attendance issues around if they are not present at their counselling sessions! It is likely to be more useful to put some energy into helping staff refer pupils to counselling earlier on, when attendance is just beginning to fall off, rather than to take on cases when matters have already progressed too far.

## Is this case suitable for this counsellor?

Beyond the general issue of whether counselling or some other approach is indicated, there is a more particular level of assessment required, relating to the training, experience and skill of the particular counsellor. A case that might be manageable for a counsellor with several years of experience after specialist training might be inappropriate for a newly qualified counsellor or one working in an unfamiliar setting or with a different client group. We need to be responsible about the cases we take on. We need to be aware of our own limitations and take care not to work beyond them. This may also arise if a child evokes too strongly issues of our own that we know we have not adequately worked through in our own counselling, and whom we therefore know we would be less able to help.

More prosaically it is also inappropriate to take on any case where there is a connection with this child or their family. It is far better to arrange referral to a colleague than to intervene in a case where there is any risk that professional or personal relationships in the background will compromise our view of the child or our freedom to work as the case requires. It is hard to be robust enough in taking up difficulties, if we are working with someone we are connected to, even if distantly, for example the child of a friend of a colleague. If for any reason we need too much to appear successful in someone else's eyes, we are unlikely to be effective. If we go into a piece of work with something too obviously to prove, it can deeply interfere with our capacity to think clearly and to respond to the real needs of the case.

It is at this point, when we are assessing whether we ourselves can manage to work well with a case, that good supervision is again at its most important. It could be that we need an outside perception to help us get a clear view and make this judgement.

## Is the child available enough for the work?

Let us now suppose that we have a child presenting with a problem, identifiable as their own, appropriately referred for counselling and within our competence. The assessment is still in its early stages. We now need to work out if this child can manage the encounter in the room sufficiently to make use of counselling. Are they willing to think about themselves at all? Are they able to tolerate us thinking about them? We might try out a few attempts at thinking out loud with them to see how they respond, and to see if they show any interest in this way of functioning. If they do not, it does not mean that we cannot start the work, but we need to have some minimal sense that they can be engageable in order to propose a longer relationship. We may think we can get through to any child who comes to us, and indeed if they keep coming we might be able to make some headway eventually with the toughest of defences, but we also need to be reasonable about the shortage of resources. If there is a long waiting list of children then it can be a counterproductive act of heroism to take on a child who is going to need many terms of work to make any kind of relationship with, if we could be working with someone who can more readily make use of us. There will need to be a complex weighing up of the severity of the problem, the degree of difficulty presented in engagement, the other possibilities that the child might take to more readily and the availability of counselling time, before a decision can be made as to whether to persevere. Sometimes in such cases an extended assessment of six or so sessions can be a good strategy, so as to get more of a sense of whether engagement will be possible and/or to do a piece of short-term work that itself may be of use.

## Anxieties and defences

Supposing we judge that the child is sufficiently emotionally available for the work – the assessment is still far from complete. We now need to look towards creating a psychodynamic formulation of what is troubling them. First we would want to get some idea of what the child is most anxious about. This may be clearly evident in the initial presentation, or it might be something that can only be gleaned over time. It also may not at all be what it appears on the surface.

Janet (13) presented herself as being very anxious over feuds and rifts in her friendship group. After a short while it was possible to see, and to her own surprise to acknowledge, that the key issue was actually her anxious, angry rivalry with her sister. What she was most afraid of was that her own anger and jealousy might be on the point of bursting through a carefully constructed edifice of polite defences.

In clarifying the anxieties, we will also be trying to see what defences the child is primarily using. We need to consider whether the child is mostly using denial, projection, splitting, confusion, manic activity, externalization or others. We will be able thereby to tune into the child's ways of managing their difficult feelings, and see how much these defences are helping them cope and how much they are getting in the way. Usually children need help because defences – which were put in place when they were necessary and which used to work – are now either not working or are no longer needed. Instead they are now impeding their relationships or development. We will need to get an idea of how rigid and entrenched their defences are, and how much it will cost the child to lower them.

Along with this will be the question of not just what the anxieties and defences are, but also of what nature. We need to ask ourselves whether the child is worried or anxious because of concern about damage to his own prospects or to others, and is trying to address worries and guilts about destructiveness or envious attacks. Are they primarily in trouble because of internal conflicts, a struggle between at least partially accessible different parts of themselves? These are what Melanie Klein would describe as depressive anxieties (Klein 1935), and they belong to a more emotionally mature and sophisticated state of mind where it is possible for the child to think and to cope somewhat with conflicting or painful feelings. Even if defences are strong, the scope is already potentially there for the work to focus on the internal conflicts that are just below consciousness.

Alternatively you may be dealing with a child who is mostly consumed with persecutory anxiety (Klein 1946). If this is the case the child will be more likely to feel as if he is the victim of endless unfairness, and may primarily see you as an enemy or alternatively want you to side with him against all his enemies. If he only presents either his hatred of others or the way in which others are damaging him, with no sense of any conflict being internal rather than external, then we need to think whether there is scope to address this over time, or maybe to accept that counselling may not be the right resource. With children who may be extremely prey to persecutory anxieties there is often still room to work, in that they might be able to use the counselling to work their way into a more depressive state of mind, and to establish a place within which they can begin to think. We may need to realize that our first duty is to offer containment, until such time as the anxieties become a little more digestible and thinking becomes more possible.

As indicated in Chapter 5, the developmental perspective needs always to be kept in mind. In thinking about the anxieties and the defences we will need always to be alert to how these connect to the age of our client. One dimension of all the judgements we make about how the child presents themselves will be that of age-appropriateness. This can sound prescriptive, as if there is only one way for, say, a 9 or a 16 year old to be, but it is going to be an essential aspect of the assessment to gauge whether they are more or less on track in their development, importantly delayed or prematurely precocious.

## Who am I to this child?

When a younger child comes for counselling, one of the first dimensions used to assess their functioning may be whether they can play (Chapter 7). With an older child the similar focus will be on whether and how they use words to communicate. Whatever the age group, what is key is how much in touch with himself and how able to express himself he is. However, another vital element of this is the early or pre-transference – i.e. who the counsellor is to the child (see page 18). The kind of person he feels he is talking to or in the presence of will be evident in the child's manner, both verbal and non-verbal. Are we like a teacher who is judging him, are we someone he is hopeful about, or is he mistrustful and anxious, as we are most likely to be an enemy? Is he coming to us feeling humiliated at needing help at all, is he hiding behind contempt and carelessness, so we will not see his vulnerability? Our information about this is not just derived from how he actually speaks and/or behaves, but also from the countertransference, i.e. how he makes us feel (see page 20). There will be important information contained in the way we find ourselves responding or being tempted to respond as a result of the child's communications.

## The child's inner emotional world

Who we are for the child is vital for the process of engagement (Chapter 9), but it is also central as a means of assessment, as it will be part of the answer to the key questions that will guide the work with the child – i.e. what figures, relationships and fantasies are most at work in this child's inner world. What we are looking for is a psychodynamic formulation, which pulls together the information provided in the first encounter (Hinshelwood 1991). With older children and adolescents we will hope to have learned something about the three areas of the child's life that will inform our formulation; their external world, their internal world and their relationship with us. With younger children we may not get much information about their external worlds directly from them, but the assessment will provide vital information about the second and third areas. This should give us enough information for us to come to a formulation of their internal situation, which can then guide us in our work.

Obtaining a full enough formulation may take a while, but in the first encounter we will have a chance to get some important information on the subject. We will have an idea of the patterns that have emerged in their description of the relationships around them or in their play. We will have had a chance to notice the emotional shapes and trajectories that keep appearing in their stories, whether these are told in words or played out with the toys/shown in their pictures. The early communications about this will be a vital part of understanding what is troubling the child and, just as importantly, how we will be able to use the sessions to help address his difficulties. As can be seen in Chapter 14, these early explorations can sometimes be all that is needed, but whatever the contract, the clearer we can be about the internal dynamics for the child, the more focused and effective the work will be.

## Why now?

In order to help clarify the dynamics around and within the child, one question we need to ask ourselves, and if possible the child, is why they have **now** come to counselling, or why the problems that have brought them here have erupted now. Sometimes it may be clear that a particular event has brought about the referral, but often the underlying dynamics for the problem will have most likely been in place for several years. Maybe something has happened or come to light that has brought the child for help at this moment, or caused them to engender more anxiety or disturbance in those around them. This question will usually illuminate most usefully the inner structure with which the child is functioning, as it will help highlight the area which is causing the most pressing difficulty. It may reveal the way in which defences that used to work have broken down. It may show how a precipitating event has broken through previous denial or uncovered past emotional conflicts that had hitherto been kept under control. It could be something internal to the child, maybe relating to their stage of life (Chapter 5), their educational challenges (Chapter 6) or something that is revealed when doing a family tree, such as a new relationship, a pregnancy in the family or a death, which has shaken the child's ability to cope (see Chapter 4 for examples).

## The use of assessment

By the end of the assessment period, whether this is a single session or a small number of sessions, something will have been discovered about all the above issues. It should be possible to formulate a set of answers to the questions posed in the assessment, and this will firstly indicate whether ongoing work is advisable and desirable. The assessment should also give the counsellor an idea of the landscape of the child's emotional world, and some idea of what depth and length of work is indicated. It will also give rise to a formulation that can be illuminating to look back on after some of the work has been done. It can provide a benchmark from which the progress of the work can be judged. The journey has yet to be made, but there is now something resembling a map to guide the two participants on their way.

# 16
# ENDINGS AND OUTCOMES

Children may be in counselling for one session only (Chapter 14) or in some cases for several years, with every possible variation in between. Whenever they have been attending for any substantial amount of time, the ending and the handling of it is going to provide a significant part of what can be taken away with them from the process of counselling (see Dyke 1984, on which some of this chapter is based). Endings may be long foreseen, for example when the counselling has been time-limited (Chapter 14) or when the child is leaving school. In these circumstances the work done on finishing the relationship and negotiating the separation can be of crucial importance. On the other hand, both when endings have been planned, and when they are not yet in view, circumstances may intrude, taking the child out of counselling without warning and therefore precluding careful preparation, for example if the child suddenly and unexpectedly moves school. Or after a thoughtful countdown, last sessions can get missed through illness, school events or other unforeseen disruptions. This can be painful for both child and counsellor, and the more one understands about the importance of endings the harder it can be when the ending does not go according to plan.

If one has the relative luxury of an ending that can be seen through to its proper conclusion, one is in a position to do something with the child that is of immense value – to help the child work through a parting and what this means to him in a way that is unlikely to have happened in their other relationships. This has the potential not only to help him take away the maximum benefit from the counselling itself, in that possible destructive forces aroused by the ending are minimized, but also to help him with what can for many children be so significant – their issues around their place in the minds of significant others and their capacity to manage feelings around loss.

The children in their work towards an ending of counselling have a complex task to perform. They will have many responses to losing their counselling, and working through them will enable them more fully to keep hold of what they have gained and make use of it as they carry on in life. Even if the counselling is ending with mutual agreement and on the basis of sufficiently complete work and substantial improvements made, it is still a loss. Any loss needs to be properly mourned if whatever was good in what has been lost is to be retained and made use of. By mourning, which is usually only used in relation to death, I mean the kind of conscious and unconscious readjustment necessary whenever something of importance has been lost, and the subsequent reorientation to the new reality that now includes that *absence*. This is a complex process which involves an inevitable assessment of that which has gone and of our relationship with it. A picture or internal version of it is built up and coloured both by the feelings associated with the experience or person while it was there and by our success or failure in adapting to the loss.

Ending a good experience and keeping it good in the mind is vital for healthy development but is bedevilled by many destructive factors. A child may manage his feelings about the end by minimizing the importance of the work, so that nothing significant is being lost. They may maintain they never needed to come anyway, or that it hasn't been that good, so who cares if it isn't there any more? Or they might take charge of the ending, so as not to feel left themselves, by leaving us instead. They can avoid the final session(s) and thereby take some bit of control left over the separation process by which in other parts of their life they have perhaps been deeply hurt. Raoul (7), for example, reversed the ending process by barricading the door in a way that kept the counsellor outside. In this way he was in possession of the room and in a position to make her the one left out. He was not getting the counselling, but no-one could say that anyone else had finished anything on him. Sadiq took this further in his last session, choosing not to attend because there was a film on in class and he didn't want to miss that.

Other children set about spoiling what they have had in order to make the leaving easier. One pair of brothers seen together would often try to make a big mess as soon as their counsellor warned them of the imminent end of a session. This was better understood when the counsellor noticed that the better the session had gone the more they needed to destroy the room before leaving. Being ousted from something they felt had been good was so much harder than leaving something trashed behind. It was not simply that they were expressing anger at being made to finish, but more that they needed to make sure that they were not leaving something that seemed of any value. This kind of dynamic, if not picked up and addressed early enough, can lead to children being very destructive in their final sessions.

Masud (9) had a different tactic to manage the ending. As it neared he started to list all the exciting things he had planned for the holiday. He also spoke of how he had a bus like the one he used in the sessions at home, a lorry like that, LEGO like this and so on. He was trying to convey and to convince himself that he was not leaving anything that he did not have access to at home. This could be seen as a comfort, a way of keeping going and reassuring himself of other resources, but it could also be seen as being in the service of a more defensive manoeuvre by which he could pretend to himself that he was not going to miss anything.

A more extreme version of this is illustrated by Vincent (14), who was leaving his special school to return to mainstream, and finishing his counselling as a result. He spent his last sessions crowing triumphantly over the boys he was leaving behind and pouring scorn and hatred on the staff, the head teacher and his counsellor. What seemed particularly powerful in Vincent was his refusal to owe the school anything, to be grateful for the help given to him to make possible the move he was making. If he were to acknowledge having received something valuable, he would have to take on board feelings of inadequacy and dependence with the concomitant fear of being left wanting, of being abandoned by that which he needed. Gratitude, as Klein emphasizes (1957) is a crucial but difficult achievement for all of us, as it means allowing something good that we need to be outside ourselves, in the control of someone else and to have been received by us. Each part of this (see Chapter 6 on Learning) is particularly hard for children who have had troubled early lives.

It is important to bear in mind how many fantasies and deep unconscious fears can be stirred up by endings. Deep-seated feelings about previous painful separations and experienced abandonments will be reworked during the ending process. Despite whatever rational grasp they may have of why the ending is occurring, children can fear that we are finishing with them because they have been too much for us. They may fear they will be forgotten or replaced by new and preferred 'siblings'. They may imagine, at times on the basis of a realistic appreciation of how difficult they have been, that we will be relieved not to see them any more. They may resent us going off into what they picture to be happy holidays with perfect families (whatever the reality may be!), when they themselves face something altogether grimmer and bleaker. They are faced with the idea of being unimportant in our lives, any notion of being special threatened by the image of other children, in counselling and in our home lives, who are going to continue with us. Ending counselling brings right to the surface the children's worries about their importance in other people's lives, their fears of being unlovable, their anxieties about whether they can hang onto what they have gained and their hurt at being left. If all these can be worked with then there is great scope for the ending of counselling, not just to consolidate but to further considerably the work done.

Sometimes their capacity to manage the ending well depends on them being able to glimpse their importance to us and to let them feel that an attachment can still be valued even if it does not last for ever. Emi (6) was finishing his counselling as I was leaving and he was going to be taken on by another counsellor afterwards. He had reacted angrily on being told about this, saying 'Why did you come if you were going to go?' This was a movingly direct communication about how the offer of a relationship can be a poisoned chalice to children who have too much experience of loss. To them, losing can seem to more than cancel out any benefit from the relationship. On Emi's last day, he did not want to come at first, but his teacher persuaded him. Emi did not want me to think he was coming and followed furtively and was very annoyed when spotted. Once inside, he became more lively, spending a good deal of time banging doors noisily. He decided to sort out his tray, weeding out the things he wanted to throw away. He put what he wanted to keep very neatly in his drawer. He took his exercise book and tore out what he had done, leaving the rest to make a fresh start next term. He asked if I would come back next term with a present and became angry when I talked about it being hard to think about missing the counselling and me rather than the present. When I added that it seemed hard to think that I too might be sad about the ending of our times together, he looked up sharply, 'Don't you want to go then?' I spoke about missing him and the times we had had together. He folded up a picture he had done earlier and wrote, 'Dear Sue, I will miss you, signed his name and ran away to hide. He needed to know that he mattered before he could really allow through that the counselling and I mattered to him.

One disconcerting aspect of planned endings is that clients who have shown solid improvement can go through a disturbed period just prior to the ending that can shake one's conviction that the bulk of the work is done. This is a well-known phenomenon, first described by Freud and written about tellingly by Segal 1988. For example, Rhiannon (17) had been referred as she was very anxious and rigid, needing everything to go as predicted and stay the same or she would have something like a panic attack. Forestalling this by trying to preplan and organize everything had become a preoccupation that was quite seriously affecting her ability to function in an ordinary adolescent way. After a period of counselling she was much more relaxed and was allowing herself to take risks and letting go of her rigid controls. An ending date was fixed, by mutual consent. However, not long after the agreement to finish, she found herself getting anxious again and having to fight her wish to pin everything down as before. It was easy for both counsellor and Rhiannon to think this was an indication that she was not ready to stop the work, but with difficulty they both kept their nerve. The recapitulation of her problems turned out to be brief and – when they could focus clearly enough – different in that Rhiannon was much more aware of what was going on and able to use new resources to at least struggle with the return of her symptoms. In the last month she and her counsellor reworked all the major themes of the counselling and by the actual ending she was feeling much more secure again, having overcome the brief relapse and able to look ahead with hope.

This connects with an issue that can be overlooked. It is not always easy for us as counsellors to manage endings well for related reasons. We may have our own difficulties about separation that become a factor in the work. It is a familiar experience for beginning counsellors to forget to give children enough notice of breaks and endings, or avoid taking up the children's obvious communications about their difficult feelings about the ending. This may be caused by fear of the children's anger, or anxieties about managing their hurt and disappointment. Or it may be more about our own painful partings in the past that have been dealt with by denial or avoidance. We may find it difficult to give up the part we have played in the child's life, despite knowing that it is time for them to move on, and to 'hand them back' to the other adults in their network. On a more straightforward level we can feel genuinely sad at the end of a piece of work, as it has been important to us as well as to the child and a real relationship has been created. In some circumstances we may feel guilty about finishing with a child, especially if the ending is not related directly to their having made all the hoped-for progress or if it is imposed from outside. We may fear that all our good work will be undone, which may have some basis but might also be somewhat omnipotent and rivalrous with the others in the child's life. It also underestimates the capacity that the children, notwithstanding all the above, can and usually do hang on to the improvements made and continue the internal work we have started.

The end of a piece of work also faces us with the need to assess our own performance as counsellors. Once it is over its successes and failures can be judged. We have to face up to the fact that there will be no more opportunities to give that extra bit of careful attention to this particular area of the work, or to make more progress with that emotional difficulty, as we had hoped. We might as a result unhelpfully try to work more intensively and pack more into the last few sessions. This can lead us to be insensitive to the child's communications which can be seriously counterproductive, not least because it has more to do with our own needs than the child's. Or we can switch off and coast to the final session, maybe justifying this by saying to ourselves that 'there are only two more sessions left so there is no point trying to do much now.' It is imperative that we work hard on our own attitudes and responses towards finishing in order to give the child the best possible opportunity to end well.

However the child reacts to the endings, our ability to tune in carefully and accurately with the emotional meaning of it to them, to spot what it throws up for them and the defences they may be using to manage it will be crucial in our helping them to leave well and to hold on to the benefits of the work.

This leads us to look into the issue of endings from a different angle. Thus far this chapter has been about the emotional experience and importance of endings, rather than about the different but related area of outcomes. It has been mentioned already that ending contains and implies the possibility of emotional evaluation and judgement. However, at a practical level, assessment of what the counselling has achieved is also an essential piece of the work of the ending process. Part of discussing the ending with a child is likely to involve a reflection with the child on what they think was useful or important for them about the counselling. We will have our initial formulations to look back on and to compare with how the child is now. The older the child, the easier it is for us to sensitively explore their initial expectations, how they experienced the sessions and what they feel they got out of counselling. With very young children, we may be in a position to focus on a number of features of the sessions and, based on this, assess the areas in which there are signs of improvement. This might include themes such as ability to use play or art; their capacity to engage with and the nature of the relationship with us; their ability to think about and reflect on their feelings and own behaviour; and capacity to tolerate frustration and emotional pain.

To assess outcomes, meetings may also be arranged with teachers and parents/carers who will give their feedback on any changes they have noticed and the ways in which they think the counselling has helped the child or young person. Or the child can be interviewed by someone other than the counsellor with a view to finding out how they have experienced the counselling and how much it has helped. These statements can then be analysed to give feedback on the nature and extent of the changes brought about by the counselling. Evaluation should always be an important part of completing a piece of work and is an essential feature of managing endings.

Another approach to presenting outcomes to employers and funders is to provide a dossier of case studies which illustrate the ways in which particular children have been helped. This is often the most emotionally powerful way of conveying the impact of the work (P2B 2007, 2008), but it does not have the empirical value of a more numerical study. Such an approach, while validly illustrating the way psychodynamic counselling has made an impact on some children, can be seen as empirically suspect as it might have just left out those who have not been helped. This is always a problem with case material based research, however telling – it does not have the objectivity of measurable data. Case studies can undoubtedly be useful to show a potential school/employer/funder how the counselling works and what it can (and perhaps what it cannot) do, and has immense value in helping those around the counselling to understand more about what goes on, but it cannot stand alone as an illustration of effectiveness.

In the current climate, there is a pressing need to gather more formal evidence to demonstrate the areas in which counselling makes the most impact. It is beyond the scope of this book to go into detail about research strategies (see McLeod 2001, Roth and Fonagy 2005, Cooper 2008 and Mayes *et al.* 2008 for a description of research methodologies). However, there are a range of tools available for counsellors to use in evaluating the outcome of their work. Some agencies have devised their own detailed forms that teachers and parents/carers fill in before counselling starts and after it finishes. These can be constructed to create a thorough portrait of the child's functioning and emotional state and may include what is hoped for as an outcome of the counselling. Comparing them after the work is over can give a good idea of where there has been improvement and what has, or has not, been achieved. This needs to be accompanied by thoughtful explanation of the realism or otherwise of the expectations, and with some exploration of what factors might either facilitate or make it difficult for the child to use the help offered. The management of expectations can be a crucial factor, not just in making the desired outcomes more achievable, but also in setting the counselling in an emotionally more perceptive context.

There are other standardized questionnaires that can be used for the same purpose where appropriate. There is the Goodman (1997) *Strengths and Difficulties Questionnaire*, or the CORE framework. These can be applied by others with smaller children, but with adolescents it can be done with their own input rather than anyone else's and this can be a powerful part of the work in itself. Or a similar framework can be used with parents' and or teachers' assessment of the situation included (Boston *et al.* 1987; Boston and Lush 1994; Jarvis *et al.* 2004). Using these tools we can put together a picture of how much has changed by the end of the counselling, and build an evidence base for our intervention.

Despite the need for clear demonstrations of the efficacy of the work, it also needs to be stressed that, because of the unconscious dimensions to all aspects of the counselling, for child, staff and carers, answers to questions, interviews and questionnaires may not fully reflect the outcome. Feelings about the ending itself may make it difficult to speak about the value of the counselling, or alternatively might lead to idealization. Complex feelings about getting help may get in the way, and/or difficulties for the adults around the provision of counselling may affect their judgement. For the child, measurements that are more about the way in which the child functions are likely to be more reliable, in that they do not depend so crucially on managing a direct judgement on something that has been a deeply personal experience. For staff and parents/carers such variables are more likely to be assessed in a more objective way, and so can be easier to use as measures of effectiveness.

Whilst we can demonstrate the ways in which counselling can make a difference in the lives of children and young people, psychodynamic counsellors are all too aware that many of the most valued – and valuable – aspects of their work can be hard to capture in formal research enquiries. Children and young people can experience significant internal shifts that result from having had a new relationship experience that exposes them to new ways of thinking about themselves and of identifying and expressing what is most important to them. This should and usually will be manifested in a reduction of symptom but the two may not go neatly hand in hand, and improvements may be subtle and/or delayed. Conversely it is not unfamiliar for there to be big improvements in the outside world leading to pressure to stop the work when the counsellor is aware that from what she sees in the room there is reason to think that the changes are not deeply rooted and that more work needs to be done.

It can also be important *when* the assessment is made. One study of group work showed little improvement immediately after the work finished, but the improvements became cumulatively more significant when followed up later (Kolvin 1987). Benefit, even if only short-term, is useful, but if temporary can give a false idea of long-term effectiveness, which is where one would expect psychodynamic work, tackling as it does the underlying causes of the difficulties, to offer most.

The Place to Be is a charity which offers therapeutic support including psychodynamic counselling to children in schools. They found, using the Goodman scale, highly significant improvements in the children seen (P2B 2007, 2008). There are many other studies showing that psychodynamic work helps; the research base is more in psychotherapy rather than psychodynamic counselling (Horn *et al.* 2005; Kennedy and Midgely (2007); Levy and Ablon 2009; Midgely *et al.* 2009), but there is still a vital need for more research to make the evidence base more solid and well-demonstrated. Unlike some other approaches, psychodynamic work is so dependent on the relationship formed that it cannot easily be standardized without its essence being compromised. However, it is increasingly possible to put well-designed research projects in place by which it can be shown that psychodynamic work compares well with other approaches

We need to attend carefully to the importance of being able to assess the efficacy of our work, if we are to expect schools and other agencies to employ psychodynamic counsellors. If we believe in what we do we need to be able to show that it is helpful. The increased emphasis on evidence-based practice requires and encourages us to gather and make available proof that what we do has a measurably good effect on the children. As is often stressed, there is a crucial difference between the absence of evidence of effectiveness and evidence of ineffectiveness, but there is an urgent need to collect more high-quality evidence so that we can back up our perceptions of the vital importance and value of psychodynamic work with sufficient objective facts and figures.

Therefore each psychodynamic counsellor needs to build into their thinking and practice an evaluative framework, so that services can be expanded and more children be offered this unique, and uniquely valuable approach.

# REFERENCES

Alvarez, A. (1989) Development toward the latency period: splitting and the need to forget in borderline children. *Journal of Child Psychotherapy*, **15**(2): 71–84.

Alvarez, A. (1992) *Live Company*. London: Routledge.

Alvarez, A. (1997) Projective identification as a communication: its grammar in borderline psychotic children, *Psychoanalytic Dialogues*, **7**: 754–768.

Andreou, C. (1999) Some intercultural issues in the therapeutic process. In: Lanyado, M. and Horne, A. *The Handbook of Child and Adolescent Psychotherapy*. London: Routledge.

Baradon *et al.* (2005) *The Practice of Psychoanalytic Parent–Infant Psychotherapy*. London: Routledge.

Barwick, N. (ed.) (2000) *Clinical Counselling in Schools*. London: Routledge.

Bion, W.R. (1959) Attacks on linking. *International Journal of Psycho-analysis*, **40**: 308–315. Repr. in: *Second Thoughts: Selected Papers on Psychoanalysis*, London: Heinemann.

Bion, W.R. (1961) *Experiences in Groups*. London: Tavistock Publications, repr. London: Routledge.

Bion, W. (1962a) *Learning from Experience*, London: Heinemann, repr London: Karnac.

Bion, W.R. (1962b) A theory of thinking. *International Journal of Psycho-analysis*, **43**: 306–310, Repr. In: *Second Thoughts; Selected Papers on Psychoanalysis*. London: Heinemann.

Bion, W.R. (1970) *Attention and Interpretation*. London: Tavistock Publications.

Bion, W. (1982) *The Long Weekend 1897–1919: Part of a Life*. Abingdon: Fleetwood Press.

Blundell, S. (2001) Psychotherapy with bereaved adolescents. In: Baruch, G. (ed.) *Community-based Psychotherapy with Young People*. Sussex: Brunner-Routledge.

Boston, M. *et al.* (1989) In search of a methodology for evaluation psychoanalytic psychotherapy with children. *Journal of Child Psychotherapy*, **15**(1): 5–8.

Boston, M. and Lush, D. (1994) Further considerations of methodology for evaluating psychoanalytic psychotherapy with children: reflection in the light of research experience. *Journal of Child Psychotherapy*, **20**(2): 205–229.

Bourne, H. (2003) A homosexual turns to woman. *British Journal of Psychotherapy*, **19(3)**: 349–354.

Britton, R. (1981) Re-enactment as an unwitting professional response to family dynamics. In: Box, S. *et al.* (ed.) *Psychotherapy with Families, an Analytic Approach*, London: Routledge.

Bruch, H. (1974) *Eating Disorders: Obesity, Anorexia Nervosa and the Person Within*. London: Taylor & Francis.

Canham, H. (2002) Group and gang states of mind. *Journal of Child Psychotherapy*, **28(2)**: 113–129.

Case, C. and Dalley, T. (2008) *Art Therapy with Children: From Infancy to Adolescence*. London: Routledge.

Children's Society (2009) *The Good Childhood Enquiry*. Children's Society.

Cooper, M. (1995) Moving on: group work with children forma multicultural primary school. In: Trowell, J. and Bower, N. (eds) *The Emotional Needs of Young Children and Their Families*. London: Routledge.

Cooper, M. (2008) *Essential Research Findings in Counselling and Psychotherapy – the Facts are Friendly*. London: Sage.

Copley, B. and Forryan, B. (1987) *Therapeutic Work with Children and Young People*. London: Cassell.

Coren, A. (2001) *Short-term Psychotherapy: a Psychodynamic Approach*. London: Palgrave.

Coren, A. (1996) Brief therapy, base metal or pure gold. *Psychodynamic Counselling*, **2(1)**: 22–38.

Dalal, F. (1988, repr. 2002) *Race, Colour and the Processes of Racialisation*. Sussex: Brunner-Routledge.

Dale, F. (1991) The triple burden. In: Szur, R. and Miller, S. (eds) *Extending Horizons*. London: Karnac.

Dalley, T. (1984) *Art as Therapy*. London: Taylor & Francis.

Davids, F. (1988) Two accounts of the management of racial difference in psychotherapy. *Journal of Social Work practice*, **3(3)**: 40–51.

Davids, F. (1992) The cutting edge of racism: an object relations view. *Bulletin of the British Psychoanalytical Society*, **28**:19–29.

Davids, F. (1998) Internal Racism; a Psychodynamic Perspective on Working with Cultural Difference. *The 1998 Lionel Monteith Lecture*. Lincoln Centre and Clinic for Psychotherapy. Unpublished.

DCSF (2008) www.dcsf.gov.uk/rsgateway/DB/SFR/s000794/index.shtml

DfES (2003) *Every Child Matters*. DfES.

Downey, J. and Friedman, R.C. (2008) Homosexuality: Psychotherapeutic Issues. *British Journal of Psychotherapy*, **24(2)**: 429–468.

Dyke, S. (1984) Psychoanalytic Insight in the Classroom – Asset or Liability. In: *Journal of Educational Therapy*, Vol. 1, 1986, repr. in Lo Spazio Ascolto a Scuola 2005 Cleup Padova.

Dyke, S. (1985) Getting Better Makes it Worse – Obstacles to Improvement in Children with Emotional and Behavioural Difficulties. In: *Winter, Maladjustment and Therapeutic Education*, repr. in Trowell, J. and Bower, M. (eds) *The Emotional Needs of Young Children and their Families*. London: Routledge.

Dyke, S. (1987) Saying No to Psychotherapy – Consultation and Assessment in a Case of Child Sexual Abuse. *Journal of Child Psychotherapy* **13(2)**: 65–79.

Fletchman Smith, B. (2000) *Mental Slavery*. London: Rebus.

Foster, A. *et al.* (2006) *Difference: an avoided topic in practice*, London: Karnac.

Foulkes, S.H. (1990) Access to unconscious processes in the group analytic group. In: Foulkes, S.H. and Pines, M. (eds) *Selected Papers: Psychoanalysis and Group Analysis*. London: Karnac.

Freud, S. (1905) *Three Essays on Sexuality*, SE Vol. 7. London: Hogarth.

Freud, S. (1916) *Some Character Types met with in Psychoanalytic Work: Those Wrecked by Success*, SE 14. London: Hogarth.

Freud, S. (1920) *Beyond the Pleasure Principle*, SE 18. London: Hogarth.

Gillick (1985) *Gillick v West Norfolk and Wisbech Area Health Authority.*

Goodenough, F. (1926) *Measurement of Intelligence by Drawing*. New York: Harcourse, Brace & World.

Goodman, R. (1997) The Strengths and Difficulties Questionnaire: a research note. *Journal of Child Psychology and Psychiatry*, **28**: 581–596

Gray, A. (1994) *An Introduction to the Psychotherapeutic Frame*. London: Routledge.

Guryan, J. *et al.* (2008). *Parental Education and Parental Time with Children*. Chicago: NBER.

Hartnup, T. (1999) The therapeutic setting: the people and the place: In: Lanyado, M. and Horne, A., *Handbook of Child Psychotherapy*. London: Routledge.

Heller, F. (2000) Creating a holding environment in an inner city school in Barwick. In: Barwick, N. (ed.) *Clinical Counselling in Schools*, London: Routledge.

Heyno, A. (2009) On being affected without being infected, managing suicidal thoughts in students. In: Briggs, S. *Relating to Self-Harm and Suicide.* London: Routledge.

Hinshelwood, R.D. (1987) *What Happens in Groups*. London: Free Association Books.

Hinshelwood, R.D. (1991) Psychodynamic formulation in assessment for psychotherapy. *British Journal of Psychotherapy*, **8(2)**: 166–174.

Hinshelwood, R.D. and Skogstad, W. (2000) *Observing Organisations*. London: Routledge.

Holmes, J. (1995) How I assess for psychoanalytic psychotherapy. In: Mace, C. (ed.) *The Art and Science of Assessment in Psychotherapy*. London: Routledge.

Horn, A. *et al.* (2005) Efficacy of short-term psychotherapy for children and adolescents with depression. *Praxis Kinderpsychology Kinderpsychiatry*, **54(7)**: 57–597.

Hoxter, S. (1986) The significance of trauma in the difficulties encountered by physically disabled children. *Journal of Child Psychotherapy*, **12(1)**: 87–102.

Hunter, M. (1986) The monster and ballet-dancer. *Journal of Child Psychotherapy*, **12(2)**: 29–40.

Institute for Public Policy Research (2009) *Thursday's Child*. IPPR.

Jarvis, M. (2004) *Psychodynamice Psychology: Classical Theory and Contemporary Research*. Andover: Cengage Learning.

Joseph, B. (1985) Transference, the total situation. *International Journal of Psychoanalysis*, **66**: 447–454.

Judd, D. (1989) *Give Sorrow Words*. London: Free Association Books.

Kegerreis, S. (1987) Saying no to psychotherapy – consultation and assessment in a case of child sexual abuse. *Journal of Child Psychotherapy*, **13**(2): 69–83.

Kegerreis, S. (1993) From a gang of two back to the family. *Journal of Psychoanalytic Psychotherapy*, **7**(1): 69–83.

Kegerreis, S. (2006) Working with children and adolescents – is specialist training necessary? *Psychodynamic Practice*, **12**(4): [page nos required]

Kennedy, E. and Midgely, N. (eds) (2007) *Process and Outcome Research in Child, Adolescent and Parent–Infant Psychotherapy: A Thematic Review*. London: NHS London.

Klein, M. (1923) The role of the school in the libidinal development of the child. In: *Love, Guilt and Reparation*. London: Hogarth.

Klein, M. (1935) A contribution to the psychogenesis of manic-depressive states. In: *Contributions to Psychoanalysis*. London: Hogarth.

Klein, M. (1940) Mourning and its relation to manic-depressive states. In: *Love, Guilt and Reparation*. London: Hogarth.

Klein, M. (1946) Notes on some schizoid mechanisms. In: Klein, M., *Envy and Gratitude*. London: Hogarth.

Klein, M. (1957) Envy and Gratitude. In: Klein, M., *Envy and Gratitude and other Works*. London: Hogarth.

Klein, M. (1959) Our adult world and its roots in infancy. In: Klein, M., *Envy, Gratitude and Other works*. London: Hogarth.

Klein, M. (1961) *Narrative of a Child Analysis*. London: Hogarth.

Leach, P. (2009) *Child Care Today*. London: Random House.

Levy, R. and Ablon, J. (2009) *Handbook of Evidence-based Psychodynamic Psychotherapy Bridging and Gap between Science and Practice*. Totowa: Humana Press.

Mak-Pearce, G. (2001) Engaging troubled adolescents in sex-session psychodynamic therapy. In: Baruch, G. (ed) *Community-based Psychotherapy with Young People*. London: Brunner-Routledge.

Malan, D. (1979) *Individual Psychotherapy and the Science of Psychodynamics*. Oxford: Butterworth Heinemann.

Mander, G. (2000) *A Psychodynamic Approach to Brief Therapy*. London: Sage.

Mayes, L., Fonagy, P. and Target, M. (2008) *Developmental Science and Psychoanalysis: Integration and Innovation*. London: Karnac.

McLeod, J. (2001) *Qualitative Research in Counselling and Psychotherapy*. London: Sage.

McDougall, J. (1989) *Theatres of the Body*. London: Free Association Books.

McGoldrick, M. Gerson, R. and Shellenburger, S. (1999) *Genograms: Assessment and Intervention*. London: Norton.

Meltzer, D. (1967) The gathering of the transference. In: *The Psychoanalytical Process*, London: Heinemann (repr. Strathclyde, Perthshire: Clunie Press 1979).

Meltzer, H. (2003) *Persistence, Onset, Risk Factors and Outcomes of Childhood Mental Disorders*. Office for National Statistics, Social Survey Division.

Meltzer, H. (2007) Childhood mental disorders in Great Britain: An epidemiological perspective. *Child Care in Practice*, **13(4)**: 313–326.

Midgely, N. *et al.* (eds) (2009) *Child Psychotherapy and Research: New Approaches, Emerging Findings*. East Sussex and New York: Routledge.

Miller, L. *et al.* (eds) (1989) *Closely Observed Infants*. London: Duckworth.

Miller-Pietroni, M (1999). Containment in theory and practice. *Psychodynamic Counselling*, **5(4)**: 407–427.

Moore, M.S. (1990) Understanding children's drawings: developmental and emotional indicators in children's human figure drawings. *Journal of Educational Therapy*, **3(2)**: 35–47.

Music, G. and Hall, B. (2008) From scapegoating to thinking and finding a home: delivering therapeutic work in schools. *Journal of Child Psychotherapy*. **34(1)**: 43–61.[initial/s of author, Hall, required]

Noonan, E. (1983) *Counselling Young People*. London: Methuen.

O'Connor, N. and Ryan, J. (1993) *Wild Desires and Mistaken Identities*. London: Virago.

O'Shaughnessy, E. (1992) Edna O'Shaughnessy in conversation with Jean Arundale. *British Journal of Psychotherapy*, **20(4)**: 527–539.

Obholzer. A. (1994) Preface in Obholzer, A. and Roberts, V., *The Unconscious at Work*. London: Routledge.

Obholzer, A. (1994) Social anxieties in public sector organisations: In: Obholzer, A. and Roberts, V. *The Unconscious at Work*. London: Routledge.

Omand, L. (2009) *Supervision in Counselling and Psychotherapy*. London: Palgrave.

Orbach, S. (1978) *Fat is a Feminist Issue*. London: Arrow.

P2B (2007) *Place to Be Journal*, London.

P2B (2008) *Place to Be Journal*, London

Parsons, M. and Dermen, S. (1999) The violent child and adolescent: In: Lanyado, M. and Horne, A., *The Handbook of Child Psychotherapy*. London: Routledge.

Pedro-Carroll, JoAnne L. (2005) Fostering resilience in the aftermath of divorce: the Role of evidence-based programs for children. *Family Court Review*, **43(1)**: 52–64.

Phillips, A. (1998, repr. 2009) *Saying No: Why it's Important for You and Your Child*. London: Faber.

Pozzi, M. (2007) *Innovations in Parent–Infant Psychotherapy*. London: Karnac.

Reid, S. (1987) The use of groups for therapeutic interventions. *Educational and Child Psychology*, **4(3/4)**: 171–179.

Reid, S. (1997) *Developments in Infant Observation*. London: Routledge.

Reid, S. (1999) Group psychotherapy. In: Lanyado, M. and Horne, A. *The Handbook of Child Psychotherapy*, London: Routledge, p. 257.

Reid, S. and Kolvin, I. (1993) Group psychotherapy for children and adolescents. *Archives of Disease in Childhood*, **69**: 244–250.

Roth, A. and Fonagy, P. (2005) *What Works for Whom: A Critical Review of Psychotherapy Research*, 2nd edn. New York: Guilford Press.

Rustin, M. and Quagliata, E. (eds) (1991) *Assessment in Child Psychotherapy*. London: Duckworth.

Ruszcynski, S. (1993) *Psychotherapy with Couples*. London: Karnac Books.

Salzberger-Wittenberg, I. et al. (1983) *The Emotional Experience of Teaching and Learning*. London: Routledge & Kegan Paul.

Scharff, D. (1982) *The Sexual Relationship*. London: Routledge.

Segal, H. (1957) Notes on symbol formation. *International Journal of Psychoanalysis*, **38**: 391–397; repr. in Spillius, E.B. (ed.) (1988) *Melanie Kelin Today, Vol 1: Mainly Theory*. London: Routledge.

Segal, H. (1988) Termination: sweating it out. Repr. in: *Psychoanalysis, Literature and War*. Papers 1972–1995. London: Routledge (1997).

Sinason, V. (1988a) Smiling, swallowing, sickening and stupefying: the effect of sexual abuse on the child. *Psychoanalytic Psychotherapy*, **3(2)**: 97–112.

Sinason, V. (1988b) Dolls and bears: from symbolic equation to symbol. The use of different play material for sexually abused children. *British Journal of Psychotherapy*, **4(4)**: 346–363.

Sinason, V. (1992) *Mental Handicap and the Human Condition*. London: Free Association Books.

Stern, D. (1995a) *The Motherhood Constellation*. New York: Basic Books. p. 19.

Stern, D. (1995b) Clinical windows into the parent–infant interaction. In: Stern, D., *The Motherhood Constellation*, New York: Basic Books.

Stern, D. et al. (1998) Non-interpretive mechanisms in psychoanalytic therapy. The 'something more' than interpretation. *International Journal of Psychoanalysis*, **79**: 903–923.

Sternberg, J. (2005) *Infant Observation at the Heart of Training*. London: Karnac.

Strachey, J. (1933) (publ. 1934) The nature of the therapeutic action of psychoanalysis. *International Journal of Psychoanalysis*, **15**: 127–159.

Taylor, D. (2001) Emotional factors and continuing professional development. *Advances in Psychiatric Treatment*, 7: 9–15.

Taylor, J. and McGuire, A.J. (2003) *British Journal of Psychotherapy*, **19(4)**: 85–92.

Temperley, J. (1979) *The Implications for Social Work Practice of Recent Psychoanalytic Developments* (unpublished paper presented at Change and Renewal in Psychodynamic Social Work Oxford).

Turp, M. (2002) *Psychosomatic Health: The Body and the Word*. London: Palgrave Macmillan.

Turp, M. (2006) *Hidden Self-Harm: Narratives from Psychotherapy*. London: Jessica Kingsley.

UK Office of National Statistics (2004) www.ons.gov.uk

UNICEF (2007) *UNICEF Report on Childhood in Industrialised Countries*. UNICEF.

UNICEF (2009) *The State of the World's Children*. UNICEF.

Waddell, M. (2002) The Assessment of Adolescents, *Journal of Child Psychotherapy*, **28**(3): 365–382.

Waddell, M. (1998) *Inside Lives*. London: Duckworth.

Walker, S. (2005) *Culturally Competent Therapy*. London: Palgrave Macmillan.

Williams, G. (1991) Work with ethnic minorities. In: Szur, R and Miller, S. (eds) *Extending Horizons: Psychoanalytic Psychotherapy with Children, Adolescents and Families*. London, Karnac.

Williams, G. (1997a) Self esteem and object esteem. In: *Internal Landscapes and Foreign Bodies*. London: Duckworth.

Williams, G. (1997b) On gang dynamics. In: *Internal Landscapes and Foreign Bodies*. London: Tavistock.

Williams, G. (1997c) The no-entry system of defences: reflections on the assessment of adolescents suffering from eating disorders. In: *Internal Landscapes and Foreign Bodies* London: Tavistock.

Wilson, P. (1989) Latency and Certainty. *Journal of Child Psychotherapy*, **15**(2): 59–70.

Wilson, P. (1991) Supervision and consultation. In: Ward, A. *et al.*, *Therapeutic Communities for Children and Young People*. London: Jessica Kingsley.

Wilson, P. (2003) Consultation and supervision. In: Ward, A. *et al.* *Therapeutic Communities for Children and Young People*. London: Jessica Kingsley.

Winnicott, C. (1955) Casework techniques in the child care services. In: Kanter, J. (ed.) *Face to Face with Children*. London: Karnac.

Winnicott, C. (1963) *New Thinking for Changing Needs*. London: ASW, repr. in *Child Care and Social Work*. Hertfordshire: Codicote Press.

Winnicott, D.W. (1953) Transitional objects and transitional phenomena. In: Winnicott, D.W., *Playing and Reality*. London: Routledge.

Winnicott, D.W. (1971) *Therapeutic Consultations in Child Psychiatry*. London: Hogarth.

Young Minds Website (2008) www.youngminds.org.uk

Youell, B. ( 2006) *The Learning Relationship*. London :Karnac.

Zaphirou Woods, M (1988) Bisexual Conflict in the analysis of an adolescent boy. *Journal of Child Psychotherapy*, **14**(1): 33–50.

# INDEX